Thankful for Squanto

History: Tisquantum (Squanto) was a Native American credited with helping the pilgrims and was present for the first Thanksgiving feast. It is estimated that he was born around 1585. Englishman Thomas Hunt, who was a lieutenant of John Smith, attempted to sell him into slavery in Spain for £20. He was able to

find his way back to America, where he befriended the pilgrims at Plymouth and helped them survive in a new land. He died in 1622 of an undiagnosed illness just days after negotiating with the Wampanoag. He had spent his lifetime teaching others the true meaning of peace and friendship. We should all be thankful to him for continuing to pass that lesson down to us.

Isabelle was nervous about her first day at a new school. "What if no one likes me? What if I can't make any new friends?" she worried. Have you ever felt that same way?

Her grandpa smiled at her. He said, "When Squanto met new people, he must have been worried too, but he didn't let that stop him from extending his hand in friendship."

"Who's Squanto?" Isabelle asked. She listened as her grandpa told the tale.

Tisquantum was a Native American of the Pawtuxet people. They ate berries, maize, and fish, and they also hunted animals for food and furs. Can you imagine what that must have been like?

Tisquantum came to be called by the nickname Squanto. When ships came to his land from England, his people traded with the strangers, giving them furs in exchange for knives, mirrors, and jewelry. One of the Englishmen was a greedy man named Thomas Hunt, who captured Native Americans to sell as slaves.

In 1614, he captured Squanto, along with many others, and took them to Spain to try to sell them. The life of a Native American in a strange land was very difficult, but Squanto did not give up hope for himself.

Squanto learned to speak English and convinced people to let him return home. For many years, he traveled around Europe, learning new skills and trying to find a way to cross the ocean to get

40 Traditional

Bed-Time Stories

for Children

with over 80 illustrations

(Black and White)

Plus 2 Bonus Stories

Bed-Time Stories with Moral Value

by

Mickey and Cavélle Roman

Arise Publishing

www.arisepublishing.com

Arise Publishing, Inc
Po Box 19816
Jacksonville, Fl 32245

ISBN-13: 978-1481860741
ISBN-10: 1481860747

Companion Books by Arise Publishing:
30 Days of Traditional Children Stories *with Illustrations*
10 National Bed-Time Stories for Children *with illustrations*
Traditional Children Stories Coloring Book
and more...

We would like to thank the following persons for their contribution to this work:

- *Rhoda Toynbee* with *Rhoda Studio* for drawing up all the illustrations and maps as well as the cover for this book
- *Loretta Campbell* for her writing and editing

Table of Contents

relationships

back to his homeland. Have you ever been far away from your home? After many years, he was able to join an expedition that was going to the New World, and he sailed for home in 1619.

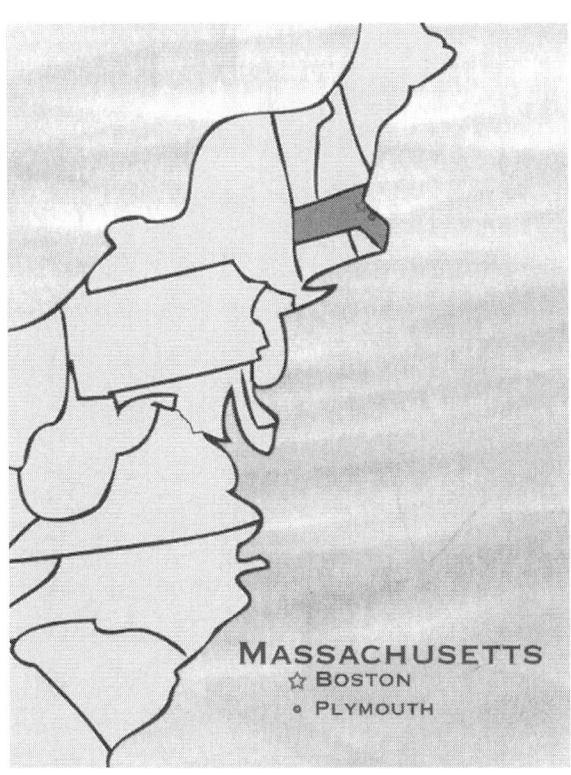

MASSACHUSETTS
☆ BOSTON
○ PLYMOUTH

Unfortunately, once Squanto got there, he learned that his entire village had been killed by a plague. There was nothing left of the village he had called home, and the English Pilgrims had built a settlement in its place called Plymouth. How do you think that made Squanto feel?

Squanto could have given up all hope then, but he did not. He went to Plymouth and befriended the people who lived there, including their town leader, William Bradford. Squanto knew that it was going to be a very cold winter and that the Pilgrims were not prepared for it. They needed someone to teach them how to survive off the land, and he needed a new place to call home.

Squanto taught the Pilgrim's that the best way to survive the coming winter was to grow maize, which is like corn and can be used to make flour. He showed them how to catch fish and use them to fertilize the maize to make it grow better. He also taught them how to catch local wildlife for food.

When the harsh snows of winter came, the Pilgrims were able to survive thanks to Squanto's teachings. Legend says that they held the first Thanksgiving feast with Squanto, and he became an important part of their community. Do you have a feast for Thanksgiving too?

Squanto became a guide and translator for the Pilgrims of Plymouth as they explored the land and tried to befriend the nearby Native Americans. One tribe, called the Wampanoag, captured Squanto to stop him from helping the colonists. A group of ten pilgrims bravely rescued him and brought him safely home to Plymouth. They knew they owed their lives to him and gladly returned the favor. How do you think Squanto felt when he was back home with the pilgrims again?

Squanto spent several years living amongst the Pilgrims and helping them, until he died of an illness in 1622, just a few days after helping the pilgrims make peace with the Wampanoag. The Governor himself, William Bradford, wrote a speech about what a great loss his absence would be. Peace between the pilgrims at Plymouth and the Wampanoag would last another fifty years, thanks to Squanto and his helpful nature. We should all be thankful to Squanto for his good heart and giving spirit. Remember to never give up in hard times and to always reach out a hand of friendship to others.

Isabelle remembered her grandpa's story of Squanto as she went to her new school the next day. It felt a lot like being with people from a new land, where she was the only stranger. Have you ever felt that way?

Isabelle saw some kids playing a game with a ball on the playground, but they couldn't win. Feeling brave and kind like Squanto, she approached them. She said, "Can I play too? I can show you a trick to help you win."

The group of children were curious to hear her advice. They let her join their game, and she showed them how to win.

"That was a great trick!" a boy named Miguel said.

"Yes!" agreed his sister, Maria. "Why don't you sit with us at lunch time, and we can all play it again!"

Isabelle happily agreed. The lesson she had learned from Squanto worked. When we extend the hand of friendship to others with a giving heart, we can make friends anywhere. Can you remember a time when you made a new friend by helping them in some way?

Bibliography:

"Native American's History, Squanto." *Mountain City Elementary School*. <http://www.mce.k12tn.net/indians/famous/squanto.htm>

"Squanto." *Wikipedia*. September 24, 2012. <www.en.wikipeidia.org/wiki/squanto>

Johnny Appleseed and Me

History: John Chapman was born on September 26, 1774 in Leominster, Massachusetts. He spent fifty years planting apple trees across the Midwest in an effort to help pioneers and to beautify the frontier. He became a legend during his lifetime

because of his generous work as a conservationist, earning him the nickname "Johnny Appleseed." He died on March 18, 1845. Memorials can be found in his honor across many of the states where he planted trees. His legend still inspires people to take care of the planet and each other. It also makes us all hunger for a fresh, crisp apple.

I was living in a little cabin with my Ma and Pa in the great state of Ohio. It was a sunny spring day in the early 1800s, and I was playing outside. Suddenly, I heard someone singing a song, and I ran through the field to see who it was. There, I saw the strangest sight I'd ever seen! It was a man wearing ragged clothes and who wore no shoes on his bare feet. On his head, he wore a cooking pot like a hat, and in his hand was a sack full of apples. His pockets were full of apple seeds, and he was planting a row of them in our field. Can you imagine how surprised I was?

"Who are you?" I asked him.

"My name is John Chapman," he said very kindly.

I knew that name from the legend I had heard. He was the one they called Johnny Appleseed! Have you heard of him too?

"Why are you planting those seeds here?" I asked him and watched as he dug a small hole in our field, carefully placing a seed in it.

He said, "Apples are a wonderful food. You can eat them, bake them into pies, or press them into cider. They also feed many animals and insects, and they are good for the earth."

"Yes, they are great," I said, "but why are you planting them here?"

He finished covering the seed with dirt and then moved down the field a little ways and began to plant another. He was planting a whole nursery of trees on our property. Ma and Pa would be so glad to see it! While he worked, he said to me, "I don't just plant them here. I come all the way from Pennsylvania. I travel to Ohio, Kentucky, Illinois, and Indiana. I plant apple trees everywhere I go."

He finished planting the last seed, humming a song as he covered it with dirt, and then he started walking down the road. I followed him.

I said "That's amazing, but I was wondering, why do you plant apple trees on land that isn't yours? Why don't you make an apple orchard of your own? Then you could sell them and be rich."

Johnny Appleseed smiled at me. He finally understood what I wanted to know. We came to an apple tree that had been badly damaged by animals. Deer had started eating the bark of the tree and hurting it. Someone had set traps around the tree and captured a rabbit. You won't believe what he did next! Johnny opened the trap and set the scared rabbit free. I guess the legend must be true. What do you think? Then he set to work building a small fence around the tree to protect it without hurting any animals.

I thought he had forgotten my question, but, while he worked on the fence, he answered it, saying to me, "I have an apple orchard of my own, and I am a nurseryman. That means I am someone who knows how to grow plants and trees, and I take good care of them. I sold lots of apples and trees, and I was very successful, but I felt most happy when I was giving away my trees for free."

We passed by some children walking, and Johnny gave them each an apple from his sack. It made them smile, and they ran home to show their Mas, laughing with joy. Have you ever given someone something like that?

Johnny said to me, "I decided to become a missionary and left my orchards for someone else to look after. Being a missionary means that I am someone who travels to far places and tries to do good work for God. I figured that the best way I could do that was to give as many people apple trees as I could. They are a big help to people starting homes on the frontier."

"So you travel all over the frontier giving away trees?" I asked, feeling impressed.

"Well, I quickly found out that it is hard to travel with trees, but it is easy to travel with seeds," Johnny said, and we both laughed.

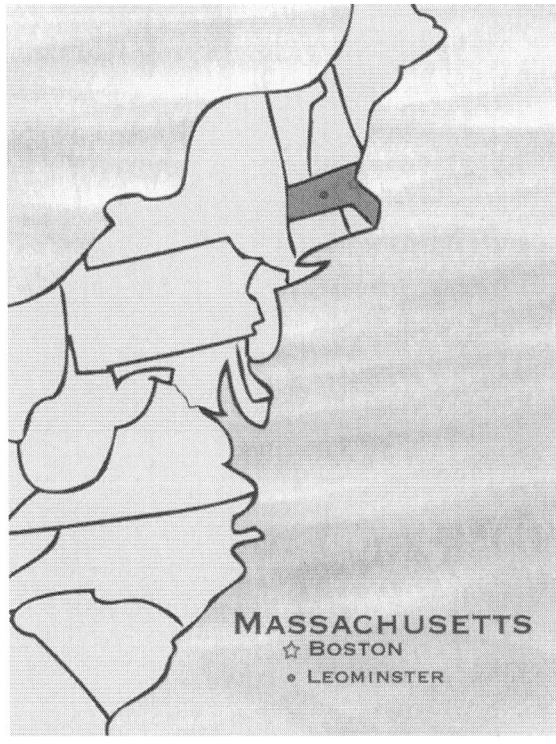

MASSACHUSETTS
☆ BOSTON
• LEOMINSTER

"So I keep my pockets full of seeds and plant as many trees as I can. I travel back to the same places I've already been so I can check on the trees I've planted and see how much they've grown."

"Why do you wear a cooking pot on your head?" I asked him. I bet you would have asked him that same thing.

"I'll show you," Johnny Appleseed said. He took the pot off his head and put several apples from his sack inside of it. Then he built a small fire and cooked the apples into a mush. He shared some with me. It was very tart but very tasty. I liked it a lot.

Then he washed the cooking pot and placed it back on his head like a hat. He said, "Now my hands are free to be able to plant more trees because I don't have to hold the pot!"

I thanked Johnny Appleseed for the yummy treat and for the wonderful seeds. He promised he'd be back one day to see how they had grown. Then he walked away on his bare feet, singing his song. I never forgot that day that I had met him, and I always took good care of the apple trees that he had given us. They provided food and cider for my family and community for a long, long, time. Have you ever a planted a tree somewhere? Johnny was right when he taught me that, if you take good care of nature, nature will take good care of you.

Bibliography:

"The Story of Johnny Appleseed," *Crispy's Apple Stand.* September 22, 2012. <www.bestapples.com/kids/teachers/johnny.shtml>

"Who Is Johnny Appleseed?" *Johnny Appleseed Junior Ecology Club.* September 22, 2012. <www.appleseed.net/about-johnny.shtml>

"Johnny Appleseed." *Wikipedia.* September 22, 2012. <www.en.wikipeidia.org/wiki/johnny_appleseed>

Helping Like Molly Pitcher

History: Molly Pitcher (Mary Ludwig Hays McCauley) volunteered to aid soldiers in the Revolutionary War and gained fame when she took up her husband's post at a cannon. The Commonwealth of Pennsylvania awarded her a pension of $40 a

year to thank her for her service in the war. Today, the United States Army has an honorary society in her name, called the Honorable Order of Molly Pitcher. It honors wives of artillerymen and recognizes people who have volunteered to improve the Field Artillery Community. Read her story to find inspiration and learn the true meaning of service, sacrifice, and why we should all be willing to do a little extra to help others.

Jason was proud that his dad was in the army, but he didn't like it when his father had to go to faraway places for many months at a time. Jason's dad said to him, "I need you to fill in for me at home and do the chores that I can't do when I'm gone. It's important that you help out when you see a need."

Jason promised his dad that he would, but he didn't want to do any extra chores. Have you ever felt this same way? His mom said to him, "Jason, can you please mow the lawn and take out the trash for me today? I already have to wash the dishes and fold the laundry when I get home from work tonight. It would be a big help if you could pitch in and do the chores your dad usually does."

Jason shook his head no. "Sorry, Mom, I can't! I'm too busy!"

Jason ran out the door and went to school. He felt a little guilty, but he didn't see any reason why he should have to do more chores. What chores do you need to do at your home?

That day in Social Studies class, his teacher Mrs. Wilson had everybody read a chapter about the Revolutionary War. Jason was impressed by the story of Molly Pitcher. Have you ever heard her story?

Mary Ludwig had been born in Pennsylvania in 1774, but everybody called her Molly. Her father worked as a butcher, and Molly stayed home and helped her mother with the household chores. In 1777, she married a man named William Hays, who worked as a barber. Her husband was against the unfair treatment of all the townspeople by the British Empire, so he became an artilleryman for the Continental Army. Molly wanted to help fight for what was right too.

Molly couldn't be a soldier in the army, so she joined a group of followers led by Martha Washington. They would travel with the soldiers and provide many important services for them. What do you think that was like?

Molly would cook and bake food for them, wash their clothes and blankets, and care for sick or wounded soldiers. When soldiers were thirsty and needed water to drink, she would bring it to them in a large pitcher. Infantry troops also needed water to cool down the hot barrels of their cannons after each shot. The men would shout "Molly! Pitcher!" giving her the famous nickname. Do you have a nickname?

Molly was very brave, carrying her water pitcher to the soldiers, even under heavy fire from the enemy in the middle of battle. She was also very strong, carrying the heavy pitcher full of water, sometimes great distances.

The Battle of Monmouth took place on a very hot day in June 1778. It was over 100 degrees Fahrenheit, and, as the battle raged, the men needed lots of water. Can you imagine how hot they must have felt?

Molly found a spring nearby and was able to use it to keep refilling her pitcher to provide them with the important water. During the battle, her husband, William Hays, was wounded. Molly watched as he was carried off the battlefield by some of the other soldiers, and she knew what she had to do!

Molly took over her husband's cannon! For the rest of the battle, Molly bravely used her husband's ramrod to swab and load the cannon. It was a difficult and dangerous job, but she saw that the job needed to be done, so she did it.

Legend says that, once, a cannon ball fired by the British flew right between her legs and tore her skirt. The legend says that Molly said, "Well, that could have been worse!" and kept right on working. Do you think you could have been as brave as her?

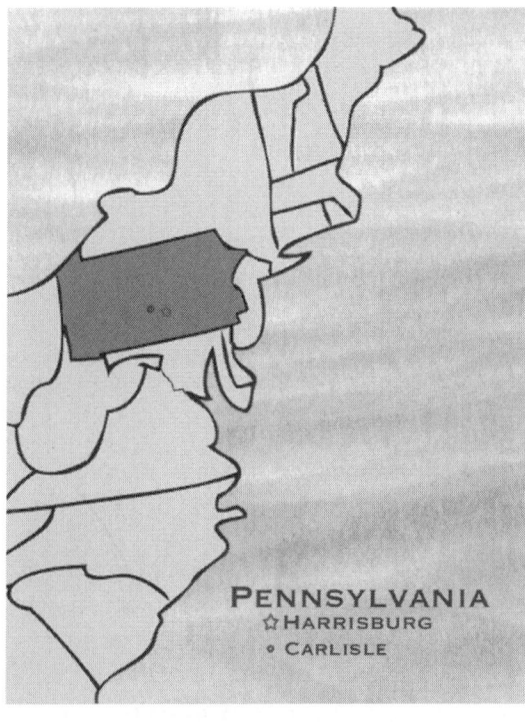

PENNSYLVANIA
☆HARRISBURG
○ CARLISLE

When night came, the British forces retreated, and the battle was considered a major victory for the Continental Army. After the battle, General George Washington asked about the brave woman he had seen loading a cannon, and everyone told him it was Molly Hays. General Washington gave her a special award for non-soldiers, and she became known by the nickname "Sergeant Molly."

When Jason got home from school that afternoon, he was still thinking of Molly Pitcher and her incredible story. She knew how important it was for someone to do chores for the soldiers, like washing their clothes and bringing them water. She also wasn't afraid to pitch in and help with a really difficult chore, like loading a cannon. Whatever job needed to be done, she was willing to do it to help. Jason realized that he was being selfish in refusing to pitch in and help his mother with the chores. What things do you think you could do to help your own family more?

Jason took out the garbage and mowed the lawn right away. When he was done, he decided to surprise his mother by folding the laundry and doing the dishes as well. When she came home from work, she was really happy and grateful for all of Jason's help. He felt good knowing that he had done his part to pitch in. He knew his dad would be happy and proud too, just like George Washington had been proud of Molly.

"Small chores are just as important as big ones," Jason said, as his mother hugged him and thanked him for his help. "When there's a chore that needs to be done, it feels good to be the one who fills that need and does it – just like Molly Pitcher!"

Bibliography:

"Molly Pitcher." *Traitors, Seamstress, and Generals: voices of the American Revolution*. September 23, 2012. <http://library.thinkquest.org/TQ0312848/mpitcher.htm>

"Molly Pitcher." *Historic Valley Forge*. *Independence Hall Association*. September 23, 2012. <www.ushistory.org/valleyforge/youasked/070.htm>

Betsy Ross and the American Flag

History: Betsy Ross was born Elizabeth Griscom on January 1, 1752. She has been credited with making the first American flag at the request of George Washington. There is no verifiable evidence that the story is true, but it has been an accepted American legend,

and it has not been discredited by historians. Betsy Ross died on January 30, 1836, and her remains have been re-interred at the Betsy Ross House, a tourist attraction in Philadelphia, Pennsylvania. Hear her story, and you will feel inspired to think about what the American flag means to you.

Jasmine sat on the couch with her grandmother, trying to learn how to get a piece of thread to go into the eye of a sewing needle. It was much harder to do than she would have thought. Have you ever tried to thread a needle?

"I can't do it!" Jasmine cried.

"Don't give up yet," her grandmother said. "Some things take a lot of patience to learn and a lot of practice to get good at. Just imagine what would have happened if Betsy Ross hadn't learned how to sew."

"Who is Betsy Ross?" Jasmine asked.

"She started out as a little girl, just like you," her grandmother said. "Her parents were Quakers. Their names were Samuel and Rebecca Griscom, and they had a total of seventeen children. Betsy was their eighth one. Can you imagine having that many brothers and sisters? When she was born, they gave her the name Elizabeth Griscom, but everybody just called her Betsy.

"As Betsy grew up, she went to a Quaker school and learned reading, writing, and sewing. When she was old enough, she left school and became an apprentice for a local upholsterer. Upholsters did all sorts of jobs involving fabric, including making furniture, sewing, and even making flags. I bet it took a lot of patience and hard work to do all those things!

"It was at her job that Betsy met another apprentice named John Ross. The members of his family were not Quakers, and he went to the Episcopal Church, which was called Christ Church. Because he was a different religion, her family would not allow her to marry him, but Betsy loved him anyway. So, one night in November of 1773, when she was 21 years old, Betsy and John Ross eloped. They took a ferry boat across the Delaware River to Hugg's Tavern and were married in the state of New Jersey. Her family, friends, and church refused to speak to her because of it, so they had to start a whole new life together.

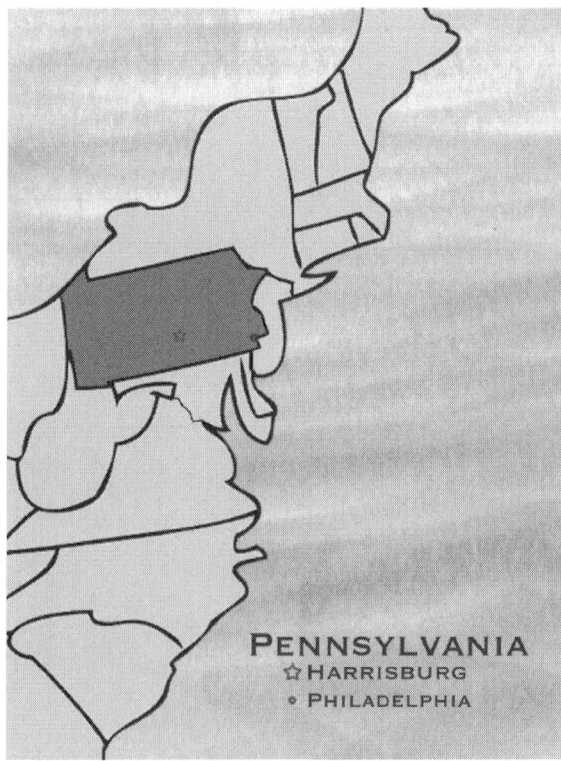

PENNSYLVANIA
☆ HARRISBURG
° PHILADELPHIA

"Betsy and John Ross started their own upholstery business together, and she started attending Christ Church with her husband. One of the people who also went to that same church was a man named George Washington, who sat on a pew very near to the one they always sat in. This was exciting because he had just been made the general of the Colonial Army, fighting for freedom in the Revolutionary War.

"George Washington would sometimes come to their upholstery shop, and Betsy would sew the ruffles on his shirts for him. Can you imagine what that would be like? This was very good for Betsy because the war had made it difficult to get fabric, so times were very hard and business was poor.

"Betsy's husband, John, joined the Pennsylvania militia and was wounded in January 1776 while guarding an ammunition cache. Betsy tried to nurse him back to health, but he died on January 21, 1776 and was buried at the Christ Church cemetery. As a young widow, Betsy upheld their upholstery business all by herself. That must have taken a lot of courage!

"Later that spring, in May of 1776, something very exciting happened that changed our country forever! George Washington himself came to Betsy's shop with two other men for a very important meeting. One of the men was Robert Morris, the wealthiest man in the colonies, and the other was Colonel George Ross, who was her late-husband's uncle and an important man in the military. I bet she was surprised that three such very important men would come into a widow's upholstery shop!

"They explained to Betsy that each of the colonies and militias had a different flag, and it was causing a lot of confusion. They needed one flag to unite them all and show Britain that they were organized and serious about fighting for their freedom. The most exciting part of all was, they wanted Betsy to sew it for them!

"They showed her a sketch they had made of what they wanted the flag to look like. As an experienced seamstress, Betsy explained to them that some changes would need to be made to give the rectangle the right shape. She also suggested that, instead of using stars with six points, they should use stars with only five points and arrange them in a circle. She knew a simple way to cut the stars, using just a few cuts with her scissors that impressed the men. They told her they wanted the colors of the flag to be red, white, and blue.

"Betsy sewed the flag for them, and on June 14, 1777 the Continental Congress adopted the National Flag. Now all the colonies would be united under the one flag, and, when anybody saw it, they would know that we were one nation! And this is all because of the hard work and dedication of a little widow who ran the upholstery shop!"

Jasmine was impressed by her grandmother's story. She never knew that a little thing like learning how to sew could have such a big impact. She was glad that Betsy Ross had sewn the first American Flag.

With new determination, Jasmine picked up her needle and her thread. She lined up the thin piece of thread with the very tiny eye of the needle and tried to get it to go through. She missed! She tried again and missed again! Jasmine remembered how Betsy Ross was able to run her own business, even after her husband had died, and she kept trying.

Suddenly, the thread lined up with the eye of the needle in just the right way, and it went straight through it! Jasmine gasped in happy surprise! She had done it! With patience and hard work, she had threaded a needle all by herself!

"I knew you could do it!" Jasmine's grandmother praised her, giving her a hug. They spent the rest of the afternoon together, and Jasmine learned how to sew a dress for her favorite doll.

Every day after that, Jasmine practiced threading a needle, and she got better and better at it. Over time, she got so good at it that she could do it without even looking! Have you ever learned to do something that took a lot of patience and practice?

Over the years, the national flag has changed and grown, just as the United States has. The most recent update to the American Flag was on August 21, 1959 when Hawaii was adopted to the nation, and the flag was given a total of fifty stars.

Since it was created, the American flag has been planted in many amazing places to show where Americans have traveled. Robert Peary climbed to the top of the North Pole in 1909 with a flag that his wife had sewn. He placed it at the North Pole then cut it into pieces and scattered it there when he left. In 1963, an American flag was placed on top of Mount Everest by Barry Bishop. There's even an American flag on the moon! It was placed there on July 20, 1969 by astronaut, Neil Armstrong. On September 11, 2001, the American flag survived the destruction of the World Trade Center, and it became a symbol of the American spirit on that tragic day.

For Jasmine, the American flag stands for patience, practice, determination. and dedication. For many people, it also stands for freedom, bravery, and sacrifice. What does the American flag mean to you?

Bibliography:

"The Betsy Ross Home Page." *U.S. History.org*. September 25, 2012. <www.ushistory.org/betsy>

The Battle of Davy Crockett

History: Davy Crockett was born August 17, 1786. He was a frontiersman, soldier, and politician. He became renowned as the "King of the Wild Frontier," attributing him with larger than life skills and making coonskin caps very popular. He represented the

state of Tennessee in the U.S. House of Representatives, fought in the Texas Revolution, and died at the infamous Battle of the Alamo on March 6, 1836. Crockett was never afraid to do what he thought was right, even against unwinnable odds. His story will inspire you to realize that, when you've done your best, you've already won – especially when it comes to helping others.

Tyler liked to do volunteer work for his school and his community. When he heard his school was having a canned food drive, he was very excited. It would be a big help to a lot of hungry families, many of whom lived in his neighborhood. Plus, whoever collected the most cans of food would win a pizza party for their class! Tyler wanted to win more than anything! Have you ever collected canned goods for a charity?

Every day after school, Tyler walked up and down his neighborhood with his Dad and asked people to donate food. Many of the people were struggling and didn't have much to spare, but they gave when they could. When the week was over, Tyler was very proud that he had collected fifty cans of food!

Tyler's friend Savannah lived in a wealthy neighborhood, and her parents had a big fancy truck. Savannah got her parents to drive her to the richest homes, where the owners donated bags full of food. One of her parents' friends owned a grocery store, and he told them to drive their truck to his shop so he could fill it with canned food as a donation!

When Tyler heard the news, he was devastated! His dad saw him looking sad, and Tyler told him what had happened.

"I'll never collect more food than Savannah now!" Tyler cried. "It's hopeless!"

Tyler's dad put his arm around his shoulder and said, "You like to help people, no matter what the odds are, just like Davy Crockett."

"You mean the kid who used to wear a coon-skin cap and hunt bears with a rifle? How am I like him?" Tyler asked.

Tyler's dad said, "The legendary folk hero Davy Crockett may have been known as *'The King of the Wild Frontier,'* but he was a lot more than a hunter and frontiersman. In real life, he was also a soldier, a legislator, and hero. He spent his whole life trying to take care of other's."

David (Davy) Crockett was born in a cabin near Limestone, Tennessee on August 17, 1786 to John and Rebecca Crockett. Families were often large back then, and he was the fifth of nine children. Times were often hard for them, and, when Davy was eight years old, he used a rifle to hunt for food along with his older brothers. Can you imagine what that must have been like? Legend says that he told his father he would be sure to make every shot count!

It has been said that he was a tough kid, standing up to bullies at school, and that he traveled the countryside from the age of thirteen to sixteen. He became very skilled at hunting and trapping animals and was especially known for trapping bears and wearing a coon-skin hat atop his head. When he was twenty years old, in 1806, he married a girl named Mary Polly Finley, and they had two sons. I wonder what it was like for his sons to have a dad who ran around with a coon-skin cap on his head.

In 1813, Davy Crockett joined the U.S. Army and served under Andrew Jackson, who later became president. They fought the Creek Indians in the southeastern plains together. When the fighting was done, Crockett's wife died in 1815, and he married Elizabeth Patton, who was a widow with two small children.

All of Crockett's adventures living on the frontier and being a soldier in the Army made him want to be a politician to make America a better place for people who needed someone to stand up for them. He was still expanding the frontier and standing up to bullies, only now he was doing it as a member of the legislature, representing Tennessee from 1821 to 1824. He went on to represent Tennessee in the U.S. Congress from 1827 to 1831 and again from 1833 to 1835.

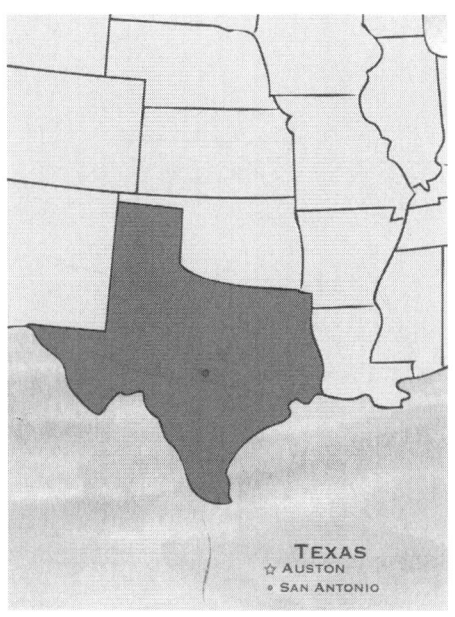

TEXAS
☆ AUSTON
● SAN ANTONIO

In 1836, he lost his bid for re-election, and his political career ended, so he packed up his family and moved to Texas, which wasn't a state yet. His heart still longed to stand up for people who needed help, and he knew that Texas was in a war for its independence from Mexico.

Crockett volunteered to go to the Alamo to help, not realizing that the Battle of the Alamo on March 6, 1836 would end his life. Historians estimate that there were only about 100 Texans in the Alamo when about 1,500 soldiers of the Mexican army attacked them. Can you imagine fighting a battle like that? Talk about hopeless odds!

It was reported that Davy Crockett fought with his rifle with amazing accuracy, skill, and bravery trying to defend the Alamo. The Texans were able to kill between 400 and 600 members of the attacking army, but they did not have enough ammunition to defend themselves from so many more advancing troops. Reinforcements of only 100 more men came to help, and so the Mexican Army overtook them and Davy Crockett was killed at the age of forty-nine.

The phrase, "Remember the Alamo," became a battle cry used by Sam Houston when he defeated the Mexican Army a few weeks later on April 21, 1836, winning independence for Texas and eventually leading to it becoming a part of the United States on December 29, 1845. Davy Crockett didn't win the battle of Alamo, but he still made an important contribution to the war that led to our eventual victory. If it hadn't been for him and what he did that day, Texas might not be a part of America today.

"Wow!" Tyler said, looking at his dad. "I thought I had it tough when I learned that I only had fifty cans of food and Savannah had thousands, but if Davy Crockett kept fighting against impossible odds, I guess I can't give up either!"

That evening, Tyler and his dad went out and collected as many canned goods as they could, even though they knew they had no chance of winning the contest. They knew they were still doing a good deed by collecting food for the needy, and they would be providing meals for the hungry, even if he didn't win the contest. What can you do to help people in your community?

Bibliography:

"Davy Crockett." *Wikipedia*. September 28, 2012. <http://en.wikipedia.org/wiki/Davy_Crockett>

The Mice and the Statue of Liberty

History: The Statue of Liberty is a colossal sculpture representing the Roman goddess of freedom holding a torch and a tablet of laws. The date of the American Declaration of Independence is inscribed on the tablet, July 4, 1776. A broken

chain lies at her feet. She is located on Liberty Island in New York Harbor, and she stands 305 feet high from the ground to top of her torch. She was a gift to America from France and was designed by sculptor Frederic Bartholdi. Building the statue was an incredible undertaking, almost as huge as the statue herself. Read her story and learn the value of hard work and the reward that comes from completing a task.

Pierre and Fifi were a pair of little gray mice. They lived in a hole in the wall of a man named Frederic Bartholdi. He was a sculptor living in Paris, France in the 1870s. Every day, the two little mice waited for the sculptor to take a break from his work so they could go looking for crumbs. Bartholdi was making a gift for the country of France to give to the United States of America. What do you think that gift was?

Pierre was so curious; he had to find out! He decided to forget looking for crumbs and take a look. Carefully, he climbed up to the top of Bartholdi's table to see what he had sketched on his pieces of paper.

Fifi stayed on the floor and kept collecting crumbs so they would have food to eat. She knew they needed to do their work first before they had fun.

Pierre looked at the sketches on Bartholdi's desk and shouted down to Fifi, "He is making a giant statue!"

"What does the statue look like?" Fifi asked, feeling curious now too. Looking at sketches sounded much more fun than collecting crumbs!

Pierre said in an excited squeak, "It is a beautiful woman dressed in long robes. There is a note written here, but I cannot read it."

Fifi couldn't resist the fun. She set down her crumbs and climbed up the table. She read the notes; they said that the statue of the woman represented Libertas, who was the Roman goddess of freedom. She explained it to Pierre, and said, "That is the perfect gift to give to America since it is known as the land of the free!"

The two playful mice looked at all of Bartholdi's sketches, running back and forth across his table with great joy. The statue's left arm was holding a big tablet of laws that had July 4, 1774 inscribed on it.

"Why does it have that date written there?" Pierre wanted to know.

Fifi knew the answer and said, "That is the date the American Declaration of Independence was signed. It is when the United States of America became its own free country."

They saw that the statue's right arm was lifting a torch high into the air. Fifi said, "I wonder why she is holding that?"

This time, Pierre knew the answer. He said, "She is enlightening the world and showing people a better way to live."

On her head, lady liberty wore a crown with seven points. Pierre said, "Maybe she has one point for each of the seven seas of the world, or perhaps it's one point for each of the seven continents."

"Maybe the points of her crown represent the rays of the sun since she's enlightening the world with both her torch and her book of laws," Fifi suggested.

"I think we're both right; I think her crown represents all three of those things together."

The playful mice noticed that the statue had a broken chain at her feet, which they both knew represented freedom. Suddenly, they heard Bartholdi coming back into his workshop, and they leapt from the table. They ran as fast as they could back to the safety of their hole in the wall, but they realized neither of them had collected any crumbs!

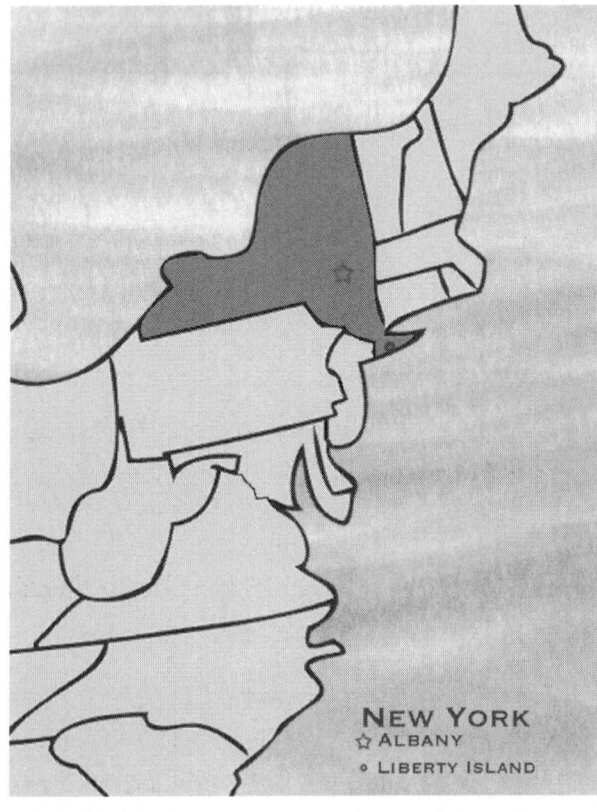

NEW YORK
☆ ALBANY
○ LIBERTY ISLAND

"I'm hungry," Pierre complained.

"Me too," Fifi said. "I guess we should have done our work first and had our fun afterward."

Pierre couldn't have agreed more! Have you ever had a time when you played when you should have done an important task? Did you learn to do your task first the next time?

Pierre and Fifi learned their lesson! Every day after that, they remembered to collect their crumbs first and save their playtime for afterward. For fun, they continued to watch Bartholdi work on building the Statue of Liberty. He used his mother as his model for making the face of the statue. When the head was completed, it was put on display at the World's Fair in Paris in 1878 to help raise money to build the rest of the statue. The fair had the best crumbs they had ever tasted!

"It's going to take a lot of money to build a statue that big!" Fifi said, as she watched someone make a donation. They dropped a piece of bread as they walked by, and Fifi eagerly grabbed it with her paws.

Pierre tried to grab a piece of cheese and was almost stepped on by a man with heavy shoes. He ducked out of the way and said, "Not only do they have to buy the materials and hire workers to build the statue, but they also have to ship it all the way across the ocean to America and pay more workers to assemble it."

Suddenly, a fat pigeon flew down and plucked up Pierre's piece of cheese with its beak, flying away just moments before Pierre could grab it.

Fifi smiled at her friend and gave him half of her piece of bread. The two mice sat side by side and shared their lunch together. What's your favorite food to share with a friend?

The two little mice watched for twenty years, as work on the enormous statue progressed. Bartholdi got a very smart engineer named Alexandre-Gustave Eiffel to help him work on the project. He would one day design the Eiffel Tower in Paris, France. Have you seen a picture of the Eiffel Tower?

Eiffel was a very smart man who figured out how to create the steel support structure inside the Statue of Liberty that would allow them to put her copy skin on the outside. People would be able to walk inside the statue, all the way up to the top of her torch. It would be able to withstand strong winds and not crumble or break. Have you ever built a tower out of blocks to see how high you can make it before it falls down? Making tall objects can be very tricky and takes a lot of hard work!

It took over twenty years, but finally they had all 350 pieces of the statue built. Pierre and Fifi watched as workers packed the pieces into 214 wooden crates. The two little mice hid themselves in one and took the long voyage by ship across the ocean to America. They had planned ahead this time and packed plenty of crumbs, so they each had enough to eat. Have you ever taken a long trip?

The Statue of Liberty was assembled on a pedestal to greet people as they enter America. She is 305 feet and 6 inches tall from the base of her pedestal to the torch. She weighs 225 tons, and wears a shoe that is 25 feet long!

Pierre and Fifi hid in the grass as President Grover Cleveland officially accepted the Statue of Liberty on October 28, 1886.

"Hooray!" they cried together. Afterwards, they lay in the grass, relaxing. They both knew that they should collect their crumbs for the day, but neither one of them wanted to have to do their chores. It was so much more fun just to do nothing.

As they lay looking up at the magnificent Lady Liberty, they remembered how the statue had started as nothing more than a sketch on a piece of paper and how so many people had worked together over so many years to make it what it had become.

"What do you think would have happened if Bartholdi had wanted to be lazy and just play all day?" Pierre wondered. "Or if any of those workers hadn't been willing to do their share and build all those hundreds of pieces?"

Fifi knew that, if that had happened, there would be no such thing as the Statue of Liberty. She jumped up and said, "Come on Pierre! The sun is shining and the day is bright! Let's get our work done right away, and then we can play!"

Pierre jumped up and joined her. Lady Liberty looked down at the two little mice and smiled from her pedestal. She felt proud because they understood that we all have important tasks we must do, and then we can enjoy our freedoms to play in the greatest country in the world.

Bibliography:

"Statue of Liberty Facts for Kids." *Buzzle*. September 25, 2012. <www.buzzle.com/articles/statue-of-liberty-facts-for-kids.html>

"Statue of Liberty." *Wikipedia*. September 25, 2012. <www.en.wikipeidia.org/wiki/statue-of-liberty>

Sir Isaac Newton

History: Sir Isaac Newton lived from 1642 to 1727. His discoveries changed the world's understanding of science, mathematics, and the universe. He is credited with discovering gravity, and his theories are still used by the greatest minds today. At the end of his life, he moved abroad and died on March 20, 1727

at the age of 84 in Kensington, Middlesex, England. His life's story is sure to inspire the scientist in us all and make you wonder what great discoveries are still left to be found.

David loved to make paper airplanes and make them fly. He made big ones and little ones, long ones and short ones. Some of them flew very far, sailing clear across the room. Some of them flew in short circles, diving down into the carpet.

The more David played with his paper airplanes, the more he began wondering about them. Why was it that some of them flew in a long, straight line, and some of them flew in a short circle? As an experiment, David decided to try making different kinds of folds in the paper to see if that changed the way the planes flew.

Have you ever wondered what makes things work, or wanted to understand them better? Have you ever tried to make an experiment to see if you can find the answer? Well, Sir Isaac Newton did all the time!

Even when he was a child, Newton always loved math and science, although he was never considered to be a very good student in school. That was probably because he liked to spend more time on his experiments than his studies.

Even though he didn't get good grades, he loved to learn. He wanted to go to college, but his family couldn't afford to send him. He was able go to college by working. He had to run errands for the other students and sometimes even eat the leftovers of their meals for food. Unfortunately, the university he attended had to close because of an outbreak of the plague, so Newton returned home to his family.

He decided to continue studying math and science on his own. Like I said, he really loved to learn! He read and performed his own experiments, writing about them in a little notebook he kept. As a man, he made three very important discoveries within a period of a year and a half. Those discoveries changed science and how we understand the world.

The first discovery happened when he saw an apple fall in the garden. It started him thinking about what caused it to fall, and he came to the conclusion that all objects, even the sun and the planets, are effected by a force he called gravity. Before that, no one had heard of gravity or knew what it was!

His thoughts on gravity caused Newton to come up with the basic laws of motion, which are:

1. An object in motion stays in motion, unless an external force stops it.

2. An object at rest, stays at rest.

3. An object moves in a straight line, unless some force diverts it.

4. For every action, there is an equal and opposite reaction.

All this was only his first great discovery! He went on to develop two more!

Newton's second discovery was about light and its properties. Have you ever seen how a prism can make a rainbow? Well, before Newton, nobody understood how to make that happen or what it meant. After spending long periods of time experimenting in a dark room, he discovered that light can be broken into different colors, and he did a lot of studies about light. He concluded that, when something appears to be a certain color, it is because it is reflecting that color of light and absorbing the others. Until that time, nobody knew why grass looked green or apples looked red!

Newton's third great discovery was to develop a kind of math called calculus. He was only 24 years old at that time, but he didn't publish his findings until twenty years later. Another man had also made the same mathematical discoveries, and there was a debate over who had first discovered it, and who had stolen the other man's idea. Today, it has been decided that both men had been able to come to the same mathematical conclusions on their own, at the same time. It's too bad they couldn't solve the debate when they were both still alive.

David wanted to be just like Sir Isaac Newton and learn about the things that interested him by studying science and making his

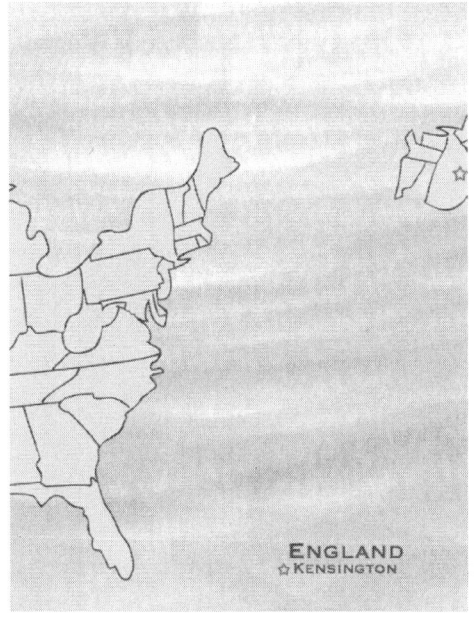

ENGLAND
☆KENSINGTON

own experiments. Maybe one day he could make a great discovery that would change the way people understand the world, just like Newton did.

How about you? Do you ever wondering what makes things work? Have you ever made an experiment to find out? Get your parents or another adult to help you find science experiments that you can do at home. Or talk to them about creating one of

your own, just like David and his paper airplanes or Newton and all the experiments in his notebook. Who knows what wonderful things you'll discover?

Bibliography:

"Biographies for Kids: Famous Leaders for Young Readers, Sir Isaac Newton." *Garden of Praise*. September 29, 2012. <http://www.gardenofpraise.com/leaders.htm>

The Wings of Freedom

History: The Bald Eagle became an emblem of the United States of America on June 20, 1782, when it was chosen by the Continental Congress to be on our Great Seal. The image of the bald eagle can be seen on the back of our gold coins, silver dollar,

half dollar, and the quarter. It has become a symbol of freedom, as its wings allow it to soar anywhere it wishes to fly. Read this story with someone you hold dear to remind them of the importance of family and forgiveness.

Every summer, Max and his family liked to go camping. There were lots of fun trails to hike and a great river they could swim and fish in. If Max caught any trout, his dad would cook it for dinner. Afterward, they would roast marshmallows over the campfire. It was always a lot of fun.

One time, Max decided to build a toy boat out of sticks to float on the river. He had just finished it and was ready to put it in the water when he noticed something sitting high on a branch up in the trees. It was a bald eagle! Sam was so excited that he called his little sister Sarah right away.

"Do you see it in that tree? Isn't it beautiful?" Max said to Sarah. The magnificent bird was easily three feet tall and very impressive to look at. "I'm going to name the eagle Freedom."

"You said it was bald, but I can see feather's on its head!" Sarah said with a confused look.

"The bald eagle isn't really bald," Max explained. "It got the name because the feathers on the eagle's head are white, but the feathers on the rest of its body are brown. Seeing a bald eagle is special, because they are the national bird of the USA."

"Cool!" Sarah exclaimed. "I'm going to tell Mom and Dad right away!"

As Sarah ran to find their parents, she accidentally stepped on something, and it made loud crunching sound. They both looked down to see that she had broken the toy boat Max had built.

Max picked it up and saw that it was broken in lots of little pieces. There was no way he'd be able to fix it. All his hard work was completely destroyed.

Max felt very angry and began to yell at his little sister, even though he knew it was an accident. She told him that she was sorry and offered to help him build a new one, but Max was too angry to hear it.

"I'll never forgive you!" he yelled. Sarah ran back to camp, crying.

"She always ruins everything!" Max mumbled to himself. He sat by river, feeling angry and upset. He picked up a small pebble and threw it into the river. It startled a fish and made it jump from the water. The eagle saw the movement with her sharp eyes and swooped down from her perch, as Max gasped in surprise at the sight. Her wings were massive, spanning seven feet across. She glided over the river, going about thirty miles per hour, reached down with her talons, and caught the fish in one easy motion. Max could hardly believe his eyes! Can you imagine how exciting that would be to see up close?

The heavy trout must have weighed nearly four pounds, but it didn't slow the mighty eagle down. Freedom simply flapped her powerful wings and flew away with her prize. Max realized the bird must have a nest nearby, and he decided to find it.

Max knew that eagles have the biggest nests of any other bird in North America and that they use the same one year after year. He had read in school that their nests could grow to be as big as 8 feet wide and 13 feet deep. Can you imagine how many sticks that must take?

After walking for a very long time, Max was becoming tired. He was just about to give up when he heard a high pitched screeching sound. He recognized the sound as being the call of the bald eagle!

He ran towards the sound, and there he saw the nest. There were two gray fuzzy baby eaglets living inside it. Although they were only four weeks old, they were already nearly a foot tall. Their mother was feeding them the last bits of the fish she had caught, and they ate it eagerly. She used her large yellow beak, which was hooked, to tear off pieces of the fish for them.

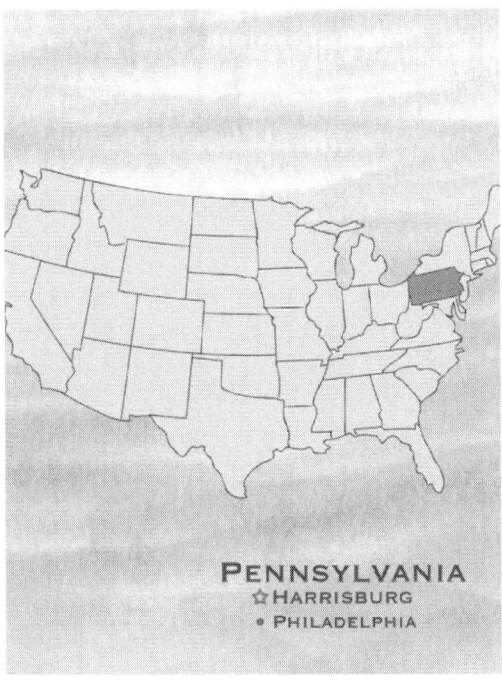

PENNSYLVANIA
☆HARRISBURG
● PHILADELPHIA

Max saw that there was another bald eagle circling the air above the nest. He realized it must be Freedom's mate, protecting their territory to keep the babies safe. Suddenly, a hawk flew into the area, and Freedom joined her mate in the sky. The two eagles worked together, fighting with their sharp talons, and drove the hawk away. It would surely remember to stay away from their territory from now on! Afterward, Freedom returned to the nest to finish feeding her babies.

Seeing the two baby birds in the nest together made Max think about his sister Sarah. He had been very hurtful to her earlier that day. He should have told her that he knew she hadn't meant to break his boat and that he accepted her apology and forgave her.

Forgiving others is an important part of being good to the people we care about. Seeing how brave, magnificent, and noble

Freedom was with her bald eagle family made Max realize that he wanted to be just as good to his own family. He had to find Sarah right away and tell her what was in his heart.

Max ran along the forest trail as fast as he could until he found Sarah.

"I'm so sorry I lost my temper and said mean things to you," he said to her. "I know you didn't mean to break my boat, and I forgive you for it. I hope you can forgive me for being mean to you about it."

Sarah hugged her brother. "I forgive you too. Maybe we can build a new boat together."

"That's a great idea!" Max said. Just then they heard the high pitched screech of an eagle. They looked up and saw Freedom and her mate flying high above them. Suddenly, two feathers fluttered down from the sky. Max and Sarah each caught one and saw with amazement that they were tail feathers from the eagles.

"I think this means they are proud of us and wanted to give us a gift!" Sarah said.

"I think so too!" Max smiled, and they waved goodbye to their new friends. What's something you can do for someone in your family to show them how much they mean to you?

Bibliography:

American Bald Eagle Information. September 27, 2012.
<http://www.baldeagleinfo.com>

Deborah Sampson

History: Deborah Sampson was born on December 17, 1760 in Plympton, Massachusetts. She longed to be a soldier and fight for our nation's independence in the Revolutionary War. Because women weren't allowed to be soldiers, she had to disguise herself

as a man. After the war, Paul Revere asked Congress to grant her a pension for her service, and she received four dollars a month. Her inspiring story serves as an affirmation that anyone, boy or girl, can do anything they set their mind to.

Has anybody ever told you that you can't do something? My name is Deborah Sampson, and it happened to me, and you'll never guess what I did about it!

I was born on December 17, 1760 in Plympton, Massachusetts. I was the oldest of six children, so I had to help my mother with my siblings a lot. One day my father, Jonathan Sampson, deserted us to become a sailor on a ship. Times were very hard for my mother after that. She soon became too poor to feed us, so she had to send my siblings and me away to live with relatives and friends.

When I was eight years old, I went to work on a farm as an indentured servant for Jeremiah Thomas and his family. The work there was very hard, but I learned to do lots of things, including riding a horse. I discovered that I could do anything I put my mind to, including sewing, spinning, hunting, and even carpentry. If something needed to be done, I could learn how to do it!

I wasn't able to go to school, but I still wanted to learn the things that other kids my age were learning. So I got the boys of the family I worked for to teach me the lessons they had learned in school. I worked for the Thomas family until I turned eighteen, and then I was released from my indentured servitude and able to get a job as a school teacher.

In 1778, the Revolutionary War broke out, and I desperately wanted to join the Army to help fight for what I thought was right. I knew I could do anything I put my mind to, but the Army disagreed. They told me I couldn't be a soldier just because I was a girl! Can you imagine that?

44

I had an idea of what I could do to fix things. Can you guess what it was? I got some men's clothing and practiced walking, talking, and acting just like a man. I got so good at it that I knew I could fool just about anybody, including my own mother. I went back to the Army and told them my name was Robert Shurtleff, and they let me join on May 20, 1782. I was chosen for the Light Infantry Company! I was a real soldier!

It was hard work being in the Army, but I'd done plenty of hard work all my life, and I wasn't afraid. I was even willing to volunteer for some very dangerous tasks. Some of the other soldiers would tease me for having a smooth face and not needing to shave, but they thought it was because I was a young boy and never suspected it was because I was really a woman.

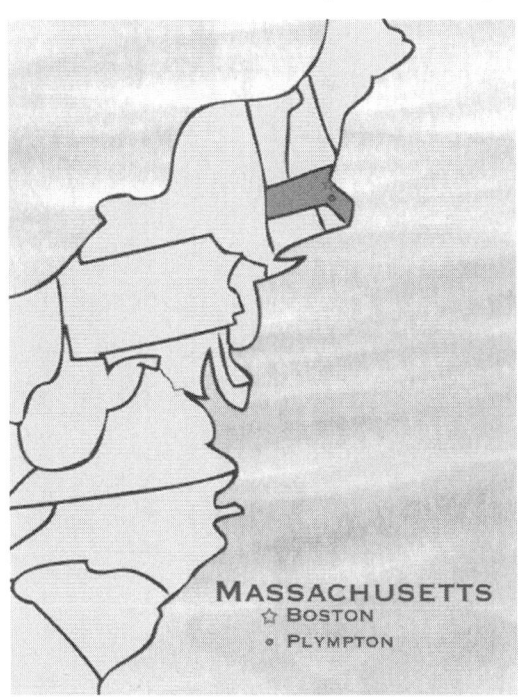

MASSACHUSETTS
☆ BOSTON
● PLYMPTON

On the fateful day of July 3, 1782, I was wounded in battle, receiving a huge cut on my head and two musket balls in my leg. I let the doctor treat the wound on my head, but not the bullet wound in my leg. I was afraid that, if I did, the doctor would discover that I was secretly a woman, and I would be killed.

I tried to treat my leg all by myself and removed one of the musket balls with a penknife and a needle, but I couldn't remove the other. Because of it, my wound couldn't heal properly. When I was able to return to service, I received a promotion and became the aid to General John Paterson. It was a great position and kept me out of any further danger.

In the summer of 1783, my wounded leg caused me to develop a horrible fever that put me in the hospital. When I awoke, I knew the doctor had discovered my secret and that he knew "Robert" was really just me, Deborah. I thought I would be in terrible trouble, but to my happy surprise I was given an honorable discharge from the Army and allowed to go home after having served a year and half as a male soldier.

Later, I met a man named Benjamin Gannett. He was a farmer, and we got married and had three wonderful children together. I got a job as a school teacher again and was often asked to give lectures about my time as a soldier. At the end of my speeches, I would dress in my uniform and give a demonstration of a soldier's routine with a gun. I think my life has been an example to many people that you can do anything you set your mind to and that it doesn't matter if you're a boy or a girl, short or tall, or young or old. We all have the ability to follow our dreams.

Bibliography:

"Biographies for Kids: Famous Leaders for Young Readers, Deborah Sampson." *Garden of Praise*. September 29, 2012. <http://www.gardenofpraise.com/leaders.htm>

"Deborah Sampson." *Wikipedia*. September 29, 2012. <www.en.wikipeidia.org/wiki/deborah-sampson>

Wright as Brothers

History: Wilbur Wright was born April 16, 1867 and died at the age of 45. His brother, Orville Wright, was born August 19, 1871 and died at the age of 76 on January 30, 1948. The Wright brothers are credited with inventing and flying the first powered, controlled

flying machine and opening the doors for modern aviation. See how the life lessons they learned can teach you to remember to always pay attention to the world around you and how the smallest observations can make all the difference.

Ricky loved to study birds. He watched them everywhere he went – at school, at the park, even in his own yard.

"Why are you always watching those stupid birds?" his brother Sam asked him one day. "Wouldn't you rather watch TV or play a video game?"

"Those things are fun to do sometimes, but you can learn a lot more by observing things around you, even birds. Just ask the Wright brothers."

"Who are they?" Sam asked.

Ricky threw some seeds out into the yard, and a tiny bird flew down to eat them, followed by another and then another. As he watched them peck at the seeds, he told his brother all about another pair of brothers who lived long ago.

"In 1899, Orville and Wilbur Wright owned a bicycle shop in their hometown of Dayton, Ohio; but their dream was to build an airplane that could fly. There weren't any planes way back then. The brothers worked on their dream constantly, testing different types of wings, engines, propellers, and controllers. They knew that, if they could just find the right combination of those elements, they could make an airplane that a man could actually fly in.

"Other men had already proven that a person could fly in the air using a glider, but no one had been able to develop an airplane that allowed the pilot to take off, control where they flew, and land safely on the ground again."

Ricky demonstrated this to Sam by making him a paper airplane and having it glide through the air. No matter how hard he tried, he couldn't control where the plane landed. Have you ever made a paper airplane?

Ricky continued his story, saying, "The Wright brothers thought they had found the solution to the problem by watching pigeons fly. They noticed that, when the birds wanted to turn, they would lift the edge of one wing up and tilt the edge of the other wing down. They started working on designing airplane wings that were flexible and could move like a birds wings."

Sam said, "Hey, they were bird-watchers just like you!"

"Yeah, but they were a lot more daring than I am!" Ricky said. He told the story about how the brothers turned a bicycle into a glider plane by attaching wings to it. "The wings had flexible flaps that could be controlled by a pilot. They took it to Kitty Hawk, North Carolina to test it because they knew there would be steady winds there to help the glider fly.

"In the summer of 1901, Wilbur acted as the pilot and made seventeen glides with their glider. The flexible wings worked and allowed him to have more control than any plane they had tried to invent before! Wilbur Wright had been able to glide for as long at twenty seconds, travelling as far as 400 feet! Now the brothers felt inspired to work even harder!

"They needed a way to test their inventions at home in Dayton without having to travel to Kitty Hawk, so they created a wind tunnel. It was made of a wood box with a fan in it that could create winds of 27 miles per hour. It was a huge help to the brothers as they tested different types of wings.

"Once they felt like they had perfected the wing design, they dedicated themselves to building propellers and a light weight engine. In the fall of 1903, they felt like they were ready, and they took their airplane to Kitty Hawk to see if they could make it work. Can you imagine how excited and nervous they must have been?

"They flipped a coin to see who would be the pilot, and Wilbur won. He layed down on the wing, grasped the controls, and took off down the starting track. The craft lifted off the ground and flew for three and a half seconds before crashing back to the ground. It took the brothers two days to repair the damages done to it, but they weren't ready to give up yet.

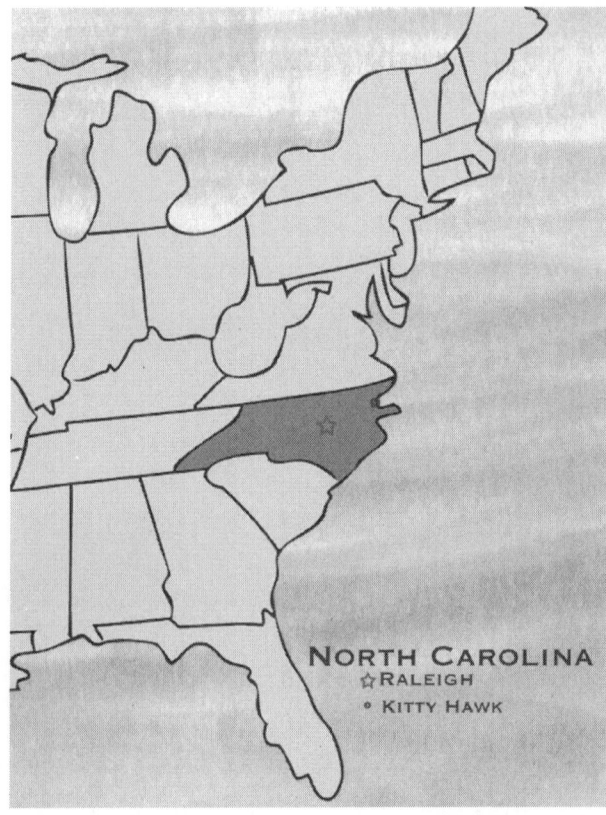

NORTH CAROLINA
☆RALEIGH
• KITTY HAWK

"On December 17, 1903, they decided to try it again. This time, it was Orville's turn to pilot the craft. It worked! The plane flew for twelve seconds and traveled a distance of 120 feet. They flew the plane a total of four times that day, with their longest flight lasting 59 seconds and traveling 852 feet. Not very far by today's standards, but it proved that it was possible to have sustained, controlled flight of an aircraft and it changed the world forever!

"Just think – all of this was possible because they'd been watching a few pigeons." Ricky smiled.

"Wow!" Sam said, grabbing a handful of seed from his brother's sack and tossing them out onto the ground. "I never realized that doing something so simple could inspire such amazing inventions."

Ricky put his arm around his brother and said, "It just goes to show you that sometimes you can learn the most from the little observations in life. So always remember to take the time each day to just look at the world around you."

Bibliography:

"Wright Flight." *PBS Kids Go*. October 1, 2012. <www.pbskids.org/wayback/flight/feature_wright>

The Wright Brothers Official Site. October 1, 2012. <http://wrightbrothers.info/>

Singing the Praises of Francis Scott Key

History: Francis Scott Key lived from August 1, 1780 to January 11, 1843. He worked as the district attorney for Washington D.C. When his friend, Dr. William Beanes, was captured by the British, President Madison allowed Key to *advocate for his release, accompanied by John Skinner, who was the Agent for the Exchange of Prisoners. The British agreed to release Dr. Beanes, but not until after the impending attack upon the city of Baltimore. So the three men were held by the British on the frigate "Surprise." Key's heartfelt poem, inspired by watching the battle, shows us all that feelings from the heart endure through all time.*

Zach and his little sister, Madison, were excited to get to go to the big game with their dad. They'd never been to a real baseball stadium before. Zach wore his baseball cap that was just like his dad's, but Maddy didn't have one, so they bought her one from a vendor. It was too big and kept sliding down over her eyes, but she didn't care. Luckily, Dad figured out how to adjust the strap in the back to make the hat fit better so she could see the game. Have you ever gone someplace special with your dad?

When the players came out on the field, everyone clapped and shouted really loud. Maddy covered her ears, and Zach cheered the loudest of anyone. Then, a lovely lady came out onto the field and the announcer said, "Please rise for our National Anthem."

Everyone stood up and faced the flag. The baseball players all took off their caps and placed their hands over their hearts. Everyone in the audience did too.

"What's going on?" little Maddy asked.

Zach had done this before at school. He had learned all about the American Flag and the National Anthem from his teacher Mrs. Bennett. Maddy was too young for school yet, so Zach knew it was up to him to help her out. Do you know what to do when you hear the National Anthem?

Zach said to his little sister, "The National Anthem is a special song that honors our country. When someone sings it, you need to listen quietly and take off your hat as a sign of respect. If there is a flag nearby, you want to face the flag and put your right hand on your heart as a sign of your devotion and love to your country."

Zach demonstrated, and Maddy copied him. The lady on the field sang the song beautifully, and afterward everyone cheered even louder than before. Then the baseball game started. It was a lot of fun. They ate hotdogs and cotton candy, and their team won by two homeruns. It was a really great day.

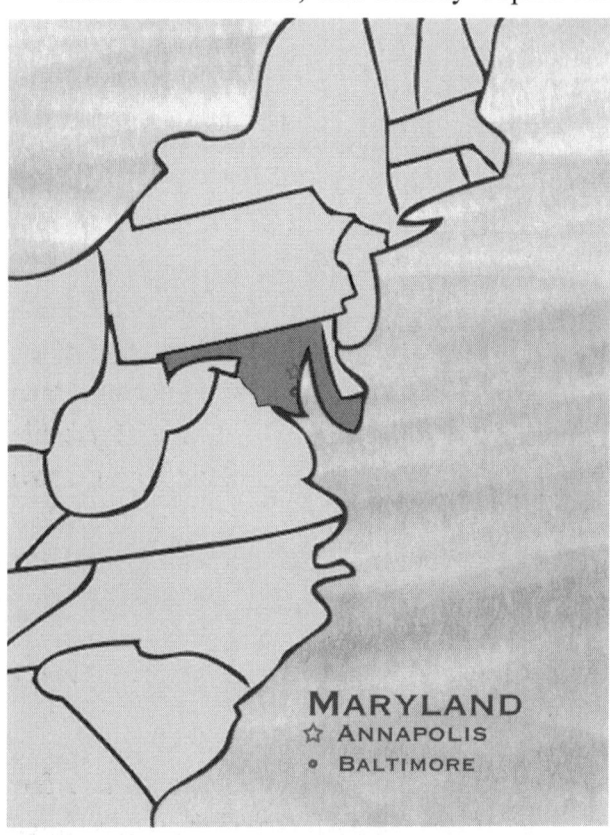

MARYLAND
☆ ANNAPOLIS
● BALTIMORE

Afterwards, as they were walking across the long parking lot to their car, Dad asked them both what their favorite part of the day had been. Do you ever play that game with your family?

"I liked it when that one player slid into home plate and knocked over the catcher, and they both got covered with dirt!" Zach said.

"That part was good!" Dad agreed. "How about you, Maddy? What was your favorite part of today?"

"I liked it when that lady sang that beautiful song at the very beginning." Maddy said enthusiastically. "Did she write it herself?"

"No, she didn't write it," Dad said. "It is a very old song. It was written by a man named Francis Scott Key back in 1814."

"Was he a famous song writer back then?" Maddy wanted to know.

"Actually, he was a lawyer in Washington D.C."

"Why would a lawyer write a song?" Maddy was curious.

Zach knew the answer to that. He had just learned about it in school. He said "The British had captured Mr. Key and put him on a ship. There was a window there, and he could look out of it and see the war going on outside. They were attacking a place called Fort McHenry. There were lots of bombs and smoke, and it was hard to see what was going on. Mr. Key knew that, when the battle was over, whichever side had won would hoist their flag to show their victory. As the sun started to rise, he stared out his window and was greatly relieved to see the American flag was waving in the air. He was so inspired that he wrote a poem about it."

"How did he write a poem if he was captured?" Maddy wondered aloud.

"He had an old letter on him, and he was able to write a few lines of his poem on the back of it. After the battle, he was released and finished writing the poem."

"So how did it get to be famous song?" Maddy asked. She was always asking questions.

This time, their dad knew the answer. He said, "Mr. Key gave his poem to a man named Captain Benjamin Eades to take to the press to be printed in the newspaper. Afterward, Captain Eades took a copy of the poem to a tavern down the street and shared it with everyone. They began to sing the poem to an old familiar tune called *Anacreon in Heaven*. The people loved the new verses and the song began to spread. It didn't take long before everyone was singing the *Star Spangled Banner*."

"Why do they sing it now at baseball games and schools?" Zach asked, having thought of a question of his own.

Dad said, "It became adopted as our country's National Anthem on March 3, 1931. Ever since then, the whole country has been singing it at sporting games, schools, military bases, and lots of other places. It's a great song, and I'm sure we'll be singing it for many generations yet to come."

"Do you think Francis Scott Key knew he was writing a song that people would be singing 200 years into the future?" Zach asked his dad, and Maddy nodded. She'd just been wondering the same thing.

Dad looked thoughtful for a moment. "I think he just wrote the poem for himself because it was what was in his heart. When you do things just to try and be famous, they can fade away quickly, but, when you do something from deep within your heart, those are the things that last."

"What do you mean?" Zach asked. Maddy leaned in close to hear, with her eyes wide. They both understood that this was an important lesson they were about to hear.

Dad held them each by the hand, one on either side of him, and said, "When you do something from deep within your heart, not to please anybody else or to try and be rich or famous, those are things that truly inspire others. Only something from the heart can touch the hearts of other people, and those are the things that people want to remember, share, and pass down through the generations."

Zach smiled because he understood. He said to his dad, "So when Mr. Key was looking for that American flag after the battle, he was thinking about his family, friends, and his love for his country; he wrote that poem with all the love for them that he felt in his heart. Then, when other people sang the song, they felt all the love for their country in their hearts too and wanted to keep singing it."

"Right!" Dad smiled back.

Maddy said, "That's why that song was my favorite part of the day today. I felt all that love for our country in it still today!"

When you hear the National Anthem what does it make you feel? Have you ever written something or drawn a picture that showed what you were feeling deep inside? If you want to make something that others will treasure forever, make it with your heart – just like Key did.

Bibliography:

"Francis Scott Key." *Francis Scott Key Official Website.* October 4, 2012. <http://francisscottkey.org/>

I'm the Empire State Building

History: The Empire State Building is an Art Deco skyscraper in New York City, stretching 102 stories into the air. It offers a 360 degree view of the city from its observation platform. It was the tallest building in the world for 40 years and continues to symbolize

the greatness of America. Enjoy a first person account from the Empire State Building itself, and learn to see the beauty and wonder where you live too.

Hello, you know me. I'm the Empire State Building. I am a 102 story skyscraper in New York City. What city and state do you live in? What's your home town like? Do you live in a city or in the country; in a house or an apartment? Is it hot or cold, wet or dry? Are there forests, oceans, cities, fields? Every hometown is different, and every one is special in its own way. I bet the place you live has many great things about it, including you!

I live in New York City in the state of New York. You can find me at the intersection of Fifth Avenue and West 34th Street in the area of Midtown Manhattan. Don't worry, I'm easy to find. After all, I was the tallest building in the world for forty years, from 1931 to 1972. I have a huge antenna spire at my top, which makes me 1,454 feet high. It acts as a lightening rod to protect me, and I get struck by lightning about 100 times each year. I got my name from where I live because New York was called the Empire State. Do you have a nickname too?

I was the first building to have more than 100 floors. You can travel to them on one of my 73 elevators, which will make you much less tired than if you take the stairs. If you do take the stairs, there are 1,860 steps to get to my top floor. It takes less than one minute for an elevator to carry you to my 80th floor, where you'll find an exhibit telling you about my construction history and a gift shop. If you travel up to my 86th floor, you'll find my outdoor observation deck, which gives you an amazing view of New York City and has been featured in several movies.

My life's not all fun and tourists, though. I have approximately 1000 businesses located inside me with about 21,000 employees. The only other building that has more employees than me is the Pentagon. I even have my own zip code, which is 10118. Do you know your address and zip code?

NEW YORK
☆ ALBANY
○ MONROE COUNTY

One of the things I was most proud of was being the world's tallest building for forty years! I received the title the day I was completed in 1931 and kept it until the World Trade Center's north tower was completed in 1972. I may have lost my title on that day, but it was fun having another skyscraper in town. I knew I had lots of advice that I could share with my new friend. Soon, the World Trade Center's south tower was completed, and they became known as The Twin Towers.

On the very sad day of September 11, 2001, the Twin Towers of the World Trade Center were destroyed in an attack. So, once again, I became the tallest building in New York, although not the tallest building in the world. I was not happy to have that title though because I would have much rather have had my friends.

On April 30, 2012, the new One World Trade Center building surpassed me. It was designed to replace the Twin Towers, and I was glad to see my friend again. The new building is more beautiful than ever before! I'm friends with the Statue of Liberty too. I hope we are all together for a long time because, when people think of New York City, they usually think of us. We're best friends forever! Do you have a friend like that too?

I love being a part of what makes New York City so great, although it's embarrassing to think of myself as an icon. To me, I'm just a place where people can work and see the city. I was built in the Art Deco Style and became a National Historic Landmark in 1986. I was named one of the Seven Wonders of the Modern World by the American Society of Civil Engineers. I don't like to brag though. The thing that makes me so great is the fact that so many great people walk in and out of my doors. Without them, I'd just be a boring, empty building.

When I was first built, I was afraid that's all I would ever be. When I first opened, it was the middle of the Great Depression, and no one could afford to rent any of my office spaces. People teased me and called me the "Empty State Building." I didn't start making a profit for my owners until 1950, and by 1951 someone wanted to buy me. I was sold to Roger L. Stevens and his partners for $51 million dollars! In 1951, that was the highest price ever paid for a building in history. I couldn't believe it!

Today, I'm a popular tourist attraction and get to see people from all over the world who come just to visit me. Over 110 million people have been to visit me so far. If you come, be prepared to stand in a lot of long lines. I'm very sorry, but there's nothing I can do about getting rid of them. My property owners make more money selling tickets to my observation tower than they do renting out all of my offices!

In 1964, I had floodlights added to light up the very top of me at night. They are beautiful, and I love using the different colors for different occasions. On St. Patrick's Day, I get to be green. On Independence Day I get to be red, white, or blue. It really gets me in the spirit of holidays! Do you dress up for the holidays too?

Sometimes, I get to use my floodlights to honor celebrities, like actress Fay Wray, who was in the movie *King Kong*. That will always be one of my favorite movies, as the famous giant gorilla climbed on top of my tower and battled against airplanes before falling to its death. Good thing that was just movie magic! That would have been really scary for me if it were real.

Sometimes, I get to use my floodlights to honor other countries. It makes me feel really special because I realize that I get to be the voice of America, speaking to our friends and allies around the world. It's a huge honor for me to get to do that. For example, on June 4, 2002, I got to become purple and gold to honor Queen Elizabeth II of England. Purple and gold are her royal colors, you know.

For fun, I get to light up in the team colors of New York's sports teams when we have home games. After all, I am a true New Yorker and have to show my team spirit! I get to light up in orange, blue, and white for the New York Knicks when they play basketball, and I wear red, white, and blue for the New York Rangers. When the U.S. Open tennis tournament takes place in Queens, New York City, I light up in tennis-ball yellow. Do you have a sports team that you like to support?

Well, it's getting late, and I have to go. Thank you for letting me talk to you about New York City and why I love it so much. Take a look at your neighborhood where you live and notice all the things about it that make you happy to live there too. America is a pretty special place to live, not just because of buildings like me, but because of people like you!

Bibliography:

"Empire State Building Facts." *Kids Can Travel.* October 7, 2012.
<www.kidscantravel.com/familyattractions/empirestatebuilding/funstuffkids/index.html>

"Empire State Building." *Wikipedia.* October 7, 2012.
<en.wikipedia.org/wiki/Empire_state_building>

Kit Carson: Legend of the Wild West

History: Christopher (Kit) Carson lived from 1809 to 1868. He served as a guide to John C. Freemont, served in the American-Mexican War, and was appointed Indian Agent in 1868. Many twenty-five cent novels were written about him, giving him

superhuman abilities and depicting him as a larger than life hero. All stories about him, whether historical or fictional, laude his great courage and goodness. Read his story and see if it brings out the best in you too.

Trevor loved to play cowboys with his friends, Mike and Luis. They put on their hats and ran around the big tree in his front yard, pretending like they lived on the frontier of the Wild West. What do you like to play with your friends?

One afternoon, Luis forgot his toy sheriff's badge when his mother called him home for dinner. Trevor really liked it. It was shiny silver and looked like a real sheriff's badge from the old west. He wanted it for himself so much, he decided to keep it. Maybe Luis wouldn't even miss it. He hid it under his bed where no one would ever find it. What do you think about that?

The next day, when his friends wanted to play, Luis asked about his missing toy.

"Have you seen my sheriff's badge? I looked for it everywhere at home, and I can't find it. I think I must have accidentally left it here yesterday."

Trevor knew he should tell his friend the truth and give him back his badge, but he wanted it so much! He knew that his mom would never be able to buy him one that looked like it. So, Trevor decided to lie. What do you think he should have done?

"No, I haven't seen it," Trevor said. Inside he felt really terrible. He knew it was wrong to steal and wrong to lie. Trevor knew that he had done both. Suddenly, he didn't feel like playing anymore.

"Your friends are outside," his mother said to him. "Don't you want to go play with them?"

"No," Trevor answered. Then he had an idea. "Mom, do you think the cowboys of the old west ever took anything that didn't belong to them or said things that weren't true?"

His mom looked thoughtful for a moment. "Well, I suppose many of them did, just like you can find many people today that steal and lie. The heroes of the old west that everyone looked up to, however, were the men who were known for their honesty, like Kit Carson."

Trevor's eyes lit up. He had heard of Kit Carson at school. "I know him! He was a trapper, scout, and a soldier of the old west! He became a legend for helping guide people through the Oregon Trail to California."

"That's right," his mom said. "Kit Carson was born on Christmas Eve in 1809 in Boone's Lick, Missouri. He didn't get to go to school very much, so he never learned to read. But when he grew up, he became a fur-trapper. He travelled throughout the west and spent a lot of time living among the Indians. He developed a strong reputation as being brave and good.

"In 1842, he met John C. Fremont, who hired him to be his guide to California. For several years, they traveled together through the Rocky Mountains and the Great Basin. John Freemont wrote many reports about their travels, in which he talked highly of Kit Carson and his courage. Soon, fictional books were written without Carson's permission, making him to be a hero capable of impossible feats. His reputation grew when he fought in the Mexican-American War of 1846, and he eventually became an Indian Agent for New Mexico until the Civil War came in 1861 and new duties were imposed upon him. In 1864, he led the conflict against the Navajo, who eventually surrendered to him and were forced to take what was called the "Long Walk," which was a 300 mile journey from Arizona to New Mexico. He retired to become a rancher and died at the age of 59, just one month after the death of his beloved wife Josephine.

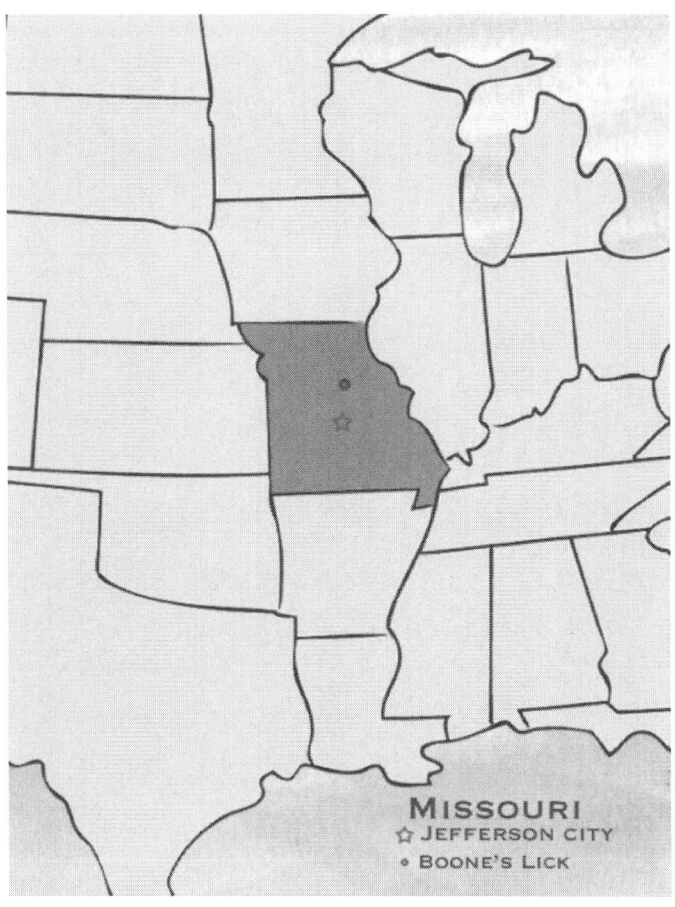

MISSOURI
☆ JEFFERSON CITY
● BOONE'S LICK

"As stories of his legend grew, everyone who read them thought Kit Carson was an amazing hero, but the people who really knew him thought he was a hero for his courage."

Tyler said, "What do you think a hero would do if he took something that wasn't his and lied about it?"

"Well, a true hero is someone who has courage. It takes a lot of courage to go up to someone and tell them that you took something from them and that you are sorry and want to give it back. It is a cowardly thing to lie and pretend like you didn't. So, I know that a real hero of the Wild West would do the brave and good thing and return the item to its rightful owner and learn from their mistake to never steal or lie again."

Tyler ran to his room and got the sheriff's badge that belonged to his friend Luis. He said to his mom, "Can I go outside and play with Luis? I have to give this back to him right away!"

Luis was so happy to have his sheriff's badge back, and he forgave Tyler right away. Tyler, on the other hand, felt relief and a sense of freedom again. What do you think you would have done in a situation like this? I'm glad Tyler learned to be honest and true, just like a real hero.

Biography:

"Kit Carson." *New Perspectives on the West*. October 5, 2012. <www.pbs.org/weta/thewest/people/a_c/carson.htm>

"Famous Leaders for Young Readers Christopher (Kit) Carson." *Garden of Praise*. October 5, 2012. <www.gardenofpraise.com/ibdkit>

Reaching the Top of the World

History: Robert Edwin Peary lived from May 6, 1856 til February 20, 1920. He is credited with having been the first man to reach the geographic North Pole of the Earth on an expedition he led on April 6, 1909. His claim was credited amidst controversy and speculation, but it played an important part in exploration

history. His persistence at realizing his dream through perseverance teaches us all to keep reaching for our goals.

Does it snow where you live? It snows where I live in the winter. I love to play in it. It's fun to make a snowman, go sledding down hills, or throw snowballs. My favorite thing to do in the snow, however, is to pretend that I am Robert Peary. He was an explorer who wanted to be the first person to reach the North Pole. It would be a dangerous and difficult journey, but he knew he could do it!

When I pretend to be Peary, I have to imagine that I am living long ago at the beginning of the 1900s. He didn't have many of the things back then that we have today. He wouldn't have had a cell phone, radio, helicopter, or the warm, protective gear we have now.

Even though he didn't have the technology of today, Peary was smart, and he studied the Inuit people to learn how to survive in very cold climates. The Inuit taught him how to build igloos. Have you ever tried to make an igloo in the snow? It's not as easy as it looks! Peary also dressed in furs, just like the Inuit did. Not only did it keep him warm, but it saved him the trouble of carrying a sleeping bag and tent. One time, I went outside dressed in my mom's fur coat, but I don't recommend doing that. She was NOT happy about it!

Peary developed a system for surviving on the long journeys that he would take, which he called the "Peary System." He would use support teams of hunters and dog sled teams to obtain food and keep it in supply caches. When he was out in the Arctic, he knew where he could always get food to survive.

Peary made his first attempt to reach the North Pole way back in 1898. During weeks of travel in extreme cold, eight of his toes froze, and he had to have them removed. Yuck! Later, he found that it was hard to walk with just two toes, so he had them removed too. I don't know what I would have done in that situation, do you?

He tried to reach the North Pole a second time and met defeat again. At the age of 25, he joined the Navy and continued to make expeditions, which allowed him to earn the rank of Admiral.

One of his trips to Greenland allowed him to make an amazing discovery. He found three of largest meteorites ever seen on Earth. One of them weighed over 65 tons! With great effort, he found a way to get them to the American Museum of Natural History in New York.

Peary gave lectures about his travels to raise money for more trips, and, by 1908, he had enough money to go on his eighth expedition and attempt to reach the North Pole. He hoped that this time he would finally succeed.

He started the journey with 23 men, but, by the time he got to the end, only five men remained, as the rest had turned back. One was an African American named Matthew Henson, and the other four were Inuits named Ootah, Egingwah, Ooqueah, and Seegloo. On April 7, 1909, he achieved his dream and reached the geographic North Pole! I love to imagine what that must have been like! I make a huge mound of snow, and I climb to the very top of it and plant a flag there. I imagine how thrilling it must have been to finally achieve a dream that I'd been working for my entire life, through freezing cold and near impossible difficulties. Have you ever tried to do something that everyone said was impossible? Have you ever tried to do something over and over, no matter how many times it took, until you finally reached your goal? It's the most amazing feeling in the world!

In the years since, there has been lots of controversy about whether or not Peary was really the first person to reach the North Pole, or if it was a man named Frederick Cook. Later, there was also suspicion that Peary's travel-mate, Matthew Henson, may have actually reached the pole ahead of him, but, if so, he never tried to take the glory away from Peary.

Peary was recognized by Congress as the first person to reach the North Pole and was given a special thanks by Congress on March 30, 1911. Peary then retired to Eagle Island on the coast of Maine, which is now a Historic Site. He died in Washington D.C. on February 20, 1920 and was buried in Arlington National

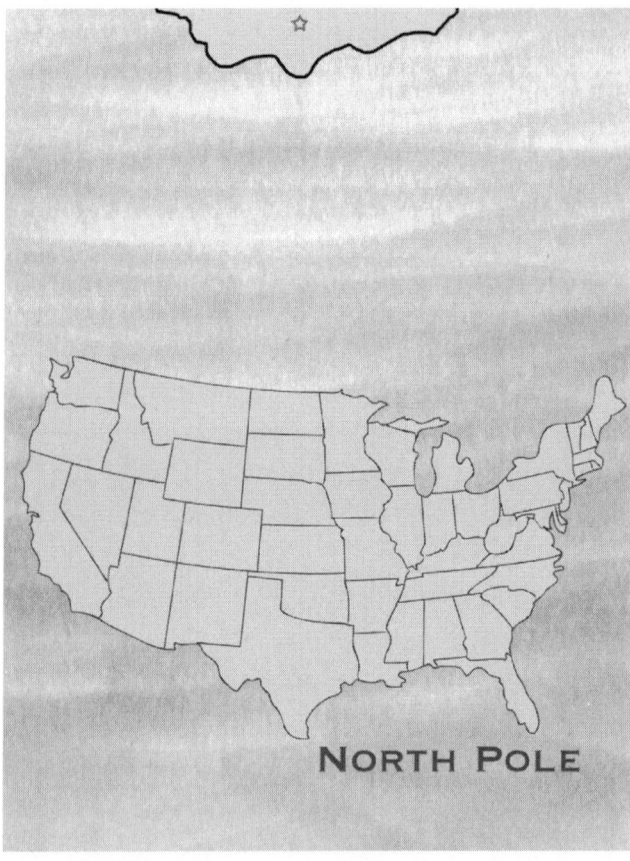

NORTH POLE

Cemetery. He worked hard his entire life to see his dream come true, no matter how long it took.

When I'm done playing in the snow and imagining I'm Robert Peary, I like to go inside my nice warm house and drink a mug of hot cocoa. It's so deliciously hot and sweet, and it warms me right up. Then I like to imagine what goals and dreams I want to accomplish.

I can't be the first person to reach the North Pole because that's already been done. Maybe I can be the first person to walk on the tip of Mars or the first person to win the science fair at my school ten times in a row! What goals and dreams do you have? Have you tried working on achieving them yet? If you try and fail, don't give up! Peary tried to get to the North Pole eight times before he made his dream come true. Just keep reaching for your goals, and you'll get there just like him!

Bibliography:

"Famous Leaders for Young Readers Robert Peary." *Garden of Praise*. October 5, 2012. <www.gardenofpraise.com/ibdkit>

"Robert Peary." *Wikipedia*. October 7, 2012. <http://en.wikipedia.org/wiki/Robert_Peary>

Helping Others with Harriet Tubman

History: Harriet Tubman was born into slavery, and her birth date is estimated to be in 1820. She escaped into freedom through the Underground Railroad and dedicated her life to helping others do the same. She was an abolitionist and humanitarian, and she

even acted as a Union spy during the Civil War. She died on March 10, 1913 at the age of 93 and is buried in Fort Hill Cemetery in Auburn, New York. Her work with the Underground Railroad is an inspiring tail of cooperation and working together to help others.

The little Blue Jay lived in a tree in Maryland and was friends with the Robin Redbreast. Each of them had a nest that they were building. Blue Jay saw a stick on the ground and wanted it for himself. Robin saw the same stick and wanted it for her own nest.

The two little birds each grabbed the stick with their beaks, Blue Jay on one end and Robin on the other. Neither bird was willing to let go. So they each pulled and pulled, just as hard as their little beaks would let them. Soon, the stick started to crack, and they realized it would break!

"We have to find a way to work together, or the stick will be destroyed," Robin Redbreast said.

"Instead of building our own nests, let's make one big one together and share it," Blue Jay suggested.

Robin agreed, and, instead of fighting over the stick, the two birds used it to begin building a large nest that they would share together. Working as a team, they discovered that the work went much faster. They didn't have to worry about fighting over sticks, and neither of them became too tired. Have you ever cooperated with someone like that?

When they were finished, they sat in their new nest to relax and watch the view of the field bellow. It was the early 1800s, and the farm land belonged to a slave-owner. The birds felt sad watching them because they knew that all people are equal and that everyone deserves to be free.

Every day, the two birds watched the slaves come out to the field to work. One of the slaves was a young girl named Harriet. She had been born around 1820, but just because she was young didn't mean she didn't have to work hard. There was never any time for her to play or even rest. When Harriet grew up, she married a free man named John Tubman. Although her husband was not a slave, Harriet still was, and she knew that, if she ever had children, they would be slaves too. She knew she had to escape! Can you imagine what that must have been like?

One evening, the little Blue Jay heard Harriett whispering with someone about running away on an Underground Railroad.

"It's not a real railroad, with trains and a track," Robin Redbreast explained to Blue Jay. "It's a secret network of houses where it is safe for a slave to hide. The slaves can go from one safe house to another until they get all the way to Canada. It's extremely dangerous for the slaves and the people helping them. Because they have to keep it a secret, they call it an Underground Railroad."

"That's a very clever idea!" Blue Jay said and flapped his wings. "They're all working together to help each other."

"Yes," Robin Redbreast agreed. "The houses where the slaves can go are called 'stations' or 'depots,' and the people who live there are called 'stationmasters.' The people who travel with the slaves and help guide them from 'station' to 'station' are called 'conductors.'"

Harriett Tubman made her plans to escape by the Underground Railroad in 1849. She left behind her husband, parents, brothers and sisters. She sang the song *Follow the Drinking Gourd* to help her remember which way to go.

"Why does she sing that song?" Blue Jay asked, as he flew overhead.

Robin Redbreast was flying alongside him and said, "The song is a code of instructions. The drinking gourd refers to the stars in the sky known as the Big Dipper. It allows her to locate the North Star, so she knows she is heading north towards Canada and doesn't become lost and head the wrong direction." Have you ever used a song to help remember something, like the alphabet or your numbers?

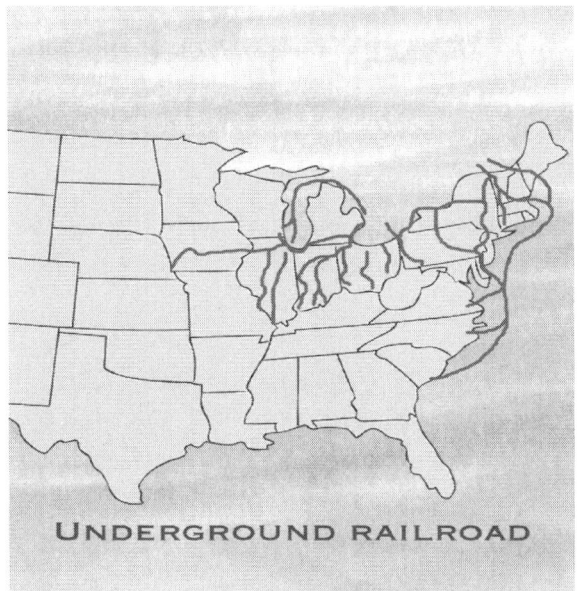

UNDERGROUND RAILROAD

The two birds followed Harriett all the way to Canada, where she was able to become a free woman. They thought that she would stay there and enjoy her new independence, but she wanted her family to be free too.

"She's going to become a 'conductor' so she can help others escape, just like she did," Robin Redbreast said, ruffling her feathers in surprise.

Indeed, Harriett went back for all her family, but she didn't stop there. She went back at least nineteen times and helped approximately 300 slaves escape to freedom.

"This is extremely dangerous!" the little Blue Jay trembled. "There is a reward for her capture of $40,000! How does she know that someone won't betray her so they can become rich?"

"Harriet may be small, but she has guts!" Robin Redbreast said, fluttering her tail. "She carries a gun for protection and won't let any of the escapees turn back. She knows that, if anyone started on the 'Railroad' and didn't finish the journey, they might tell others how to find it, and they could all get caught."

The two little birds saw that Harriett earned many friends through her travels, and no one ever betrayed her to those who wanted to capture her.

When she wanted to help her parents escape, they were too old and frail to make the trip by foot, and she needed to use a wagon. Senator William H. Seward allowed her to move her parents into a house that he owned in the state of New York. As a free woman, Harriett was able to buy that house and stayed there when she wasn't travelling with the Underground Railroad. She lived a very full life until she passed away at the age of 93 in Auburn, New York.

The two little birds built a new nest to live in near her house where they could always keep watch over her. They built the nest together, working as a team. As Harriett Tubman demonstrated her entire life, great things can happen when we all work together. Even an entire population of people can be set free.

Bibliography:

"Harriett Tubman." *History.com*. October 6, 2012. <www.history.com/topics/harriet-tubman>

Aim High Like Annie Oakley

    History: Annie Oakley was born Phoebe Ann Moses on August 13, 1860 in Ohio. She was an exhibition shooter in the Buffalo Bills Wild West show, which earned her legendary fame for her skills as a sharpshooter. She died of pernicious anemia at the age of sixty-

six on November 3, 1926 and was buried in Brock Cemetery in Greenville, Ohio. As a poor farm girl who gained star status in an industry dominated by men, she is an example to us all that we can be anything we want to be in life and no dream is impossible.

Mrs. Bennett asked all the students in her class to draw a picture of what they wanted to be when they grew up. Kyle wanted to be a doctor. He had already won first place in the science fair. Sarah wanted to be a ballerina. Her mother took her to dance class three days a week. Miguel wanted to be a soccer player. He was one of the best players on his team.

"What about you, Anna? What do you want to be when you grow up?" Mrs. Bennett asked her.

Anna looked down at the ground, feeling shy and embarrassed. She knew what she wanted to be, but she didn't want to tell anybody. She was worried that everyone would laugh at her or say she couldn't do it.

Mrs. Bennett kept encouraging her, so finally Anna decided to tell. She said, "I want to be the first female president of the United States."

Everyone in the class giggled, just like Anna had feared they would – everyone except Mrs. Bennett.

Mrs. Bennett just smiled at her and said, "I think that is a terrific goal. You remind me of another Ann in history, who was able to do things that no one thought a woman could do."

"Who's that?" Kyle asked from the back of the room.

"Annie Oakley," Mrs. Bennett said. "Does anybody in the class know who she was?"

"Sure!" Miguel cried out. "She was the girl who traveled with the Wild West show in the old days."

Sarah said, "She could perform amazing tricks with a gun, shooting things before they fell or shooting a playing card right in half!"

Mrs. Bennett said, "Annie Oakley became a legendary shooter of the Wild West, but she didn't start out that way. She started out just a regular girl like anybody else. She was born Phoebe Ann Moses on August 13, 1860 in Darke County, Ohio. When Annie's father died, her mother was unable to provide for her and her six brothers and sisters, so Annie had to go live on a poor farm. She returned to her mother when she was fifteen years old and earned money hunting animals and selling them. She got to be really good with a gun.

"On Thanksgiving Day, 1881 in Greenville, Ohio, Annie went to see the Butler and Baughman shooting act. Frank Butler was asking for challengers in a bird shooting competition and was shocked when a cute, young girl stepped up. Annie beat him fair and square, and a romance quickly developed. The two were married on June 20, 1882 when Annie was 21 years old.

"When her husband's partner became ill, Annie filled in and joined Frank in his shooting act. The crowds absolutely loved her. She gave herself the stage name Annie Oakley and began to tour with Frank. He realized that she had the talent and the personality to be a huge star and ended his own career to become her manager.

"In 1885, they joined with the famous Buffalo Bill Cody, and Annie Oakley became a part of his Wild West show. She toured with him for sixteen seasons. She could shoot with both her left hand and her right, and she hardly ever missed a shot. Frank would throw a clay bird in the air, and Annie would jump over her table and shoot the bird before it hit the ground. She was a great actress and show person, which allowed her to show off her great talent and skills with a gun.

"Buffalo Bill took his show to Europe, and Annie got to meet Queen Victoria in London. She also got to tour Paris, France. After they returned to America, Thomas Edison invented the movie camera, and he asked Annie and Frank to let him film them. It was the beginning of the era of movies, and

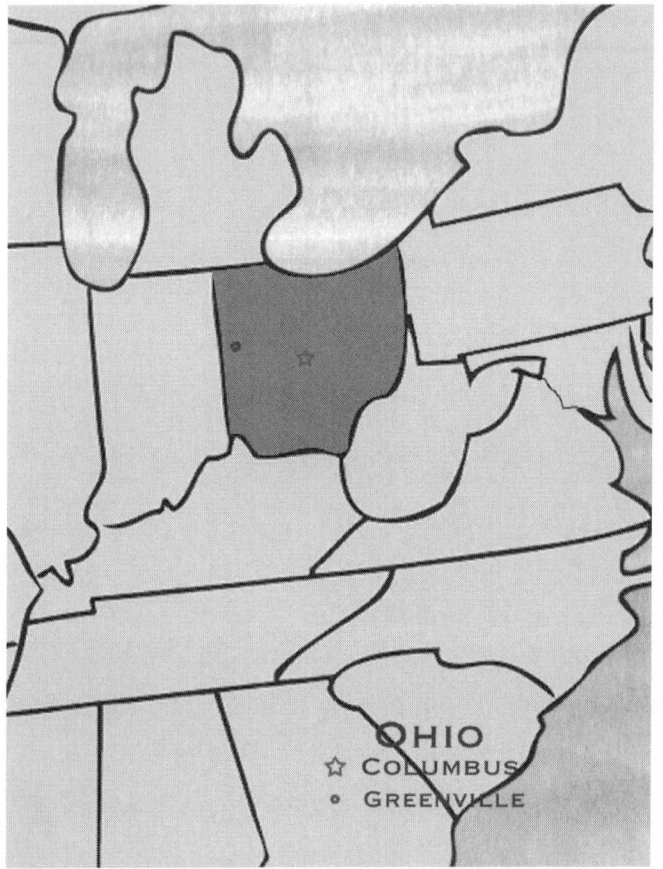

people stopped going to shows like Buffalo Bill's Wild West show. Instead, they went to see movie films.

"In 1901, Annie hurt her back in a train wreck, so she had to stop performing. During her lifetime, she was an advocate for women and thought they should all have the ability to protect themselves from danger. She taught thousands of women on how to shoot a gun. She died at the age of 66 on November 3, 1926 in her home town of Darke County, Ohio. She had lived a full and exciting life.

"So you see, class," Mrs. Bennett said as she wrapped up her story, "you can all grow up to do incredible things with your lives and be anything you want to be, as long as you're willing to work hard to get there. If a little girl from the country poor house can grow up to be a big shooting star like Annie Oakley, you too can grow up to be something amazing!"

Bibliography:

"Articles Featuring Annie Oakley." *History Net Magazines*. October 7, 2012. <http://www.historynet.com/annie-oakley>

With Clinton Fisk, Equality's Not at Risk

History: Clinton B. Fisk was born in Livingston County, New York to Benjamin and Lydia Fisk. He graduated from Michigan Central College in 1844 as one of only five students and moved to St. Louis, Missouri to work in the insurance business. After his

Floppy was a big, furry dog with long ears. He loved to go to the park and roll in the soft grass under the shade trees. Lots of dogs went to the park too. There were little dogs with pointy ears and skinny legs; there were short dogs with stubby legs and tails that were almost too short to wag; there were scruffy dogs with tongues that would hang out; and there were tall dogs with long tails that almost knocked you over if you got too close. The park was definitely the place to go if you were a dog!

Patches was a cat with soft white fur covered with patches of tan and black. He was a beautiful cat with a long fluffy tail and bright blue eyes. Patches was very friendly and loved to sit on people's laps and let them stroke his fur and scratch his ears. He was also a good hunter and could catch a mouse with one stroke of his paw or snag a bird even before it had a chance to fly away.

One day, Patches was stalking a bird through town when it flew into an area full of trees and escaped onto a high branch. Patches was good at climbing trees and followed the bird. When he reached a tall branch of the tree, Patches looked around and saw that there was a beautiful park down bellow. Patches was amazed. He had never such a wonderful place!

The park was full of trees, soft grass, and fragrant flowers.

"Wow! I really like it here!" Patches thought to himself.

A big dog named Bruno saw the colorful cat sitting on the tree branch and began to bark at him. The dog said, "Get out of here!

This park is for dogs only! We're better than cats, so only we get to use the park! You have to leave!"

Patches was frightened and ran away, but he couldn't stop thinking about the park. It was a nice place, and he wanted to get to use it too. A few days later, Patches returned to the park with several of his cat friends. They all agreed that they deserved to use the park too.

Bruno saw them and began to bark ferociously, trying to chase the cats away. Floppy heard all the noise and came to see what was going on.

"These cats don't belong in our park!" Bruno said to Floppy. "Dogs are better than cats, and we need to keep them out of our park!"

Floppy shook his head, and his tail began to droop. He said, "I don't agree with that idea at all. Cats and dogs are equal, and we should all be able to share the park together. We should all try to be like Clinton Fisk."

"Who is that?" Bruno asked. Patches and his friends listened carefully as well.

Floppy explained, "Clinton B. Fisk lived in time of slavery, when certain people didn't understand that all people are equal. They wanted to treat African Americans unfairly. Fisk thought those people were wrong. He became an abolitionist, which means he wanted to put an end to slavery.

"During the Civil War, Fisk was made a Colonel in the Union Army on September 5, 1862. He bravely commanded soldiers to block the Confederate Army from raiding into Missouri.

"When the war was finally over, he worked to establish the first free schools in the South, where white children and black children could go to school together. Until that time, all children in the South had to be separated according to the color of their skin, and they couldn't go to school together. Isn't that ridiculous? Fisk knew it was very wrong, so he turned an abandoned barracks in Nashville, Tennessee into the Fisk School, where all children could go together.

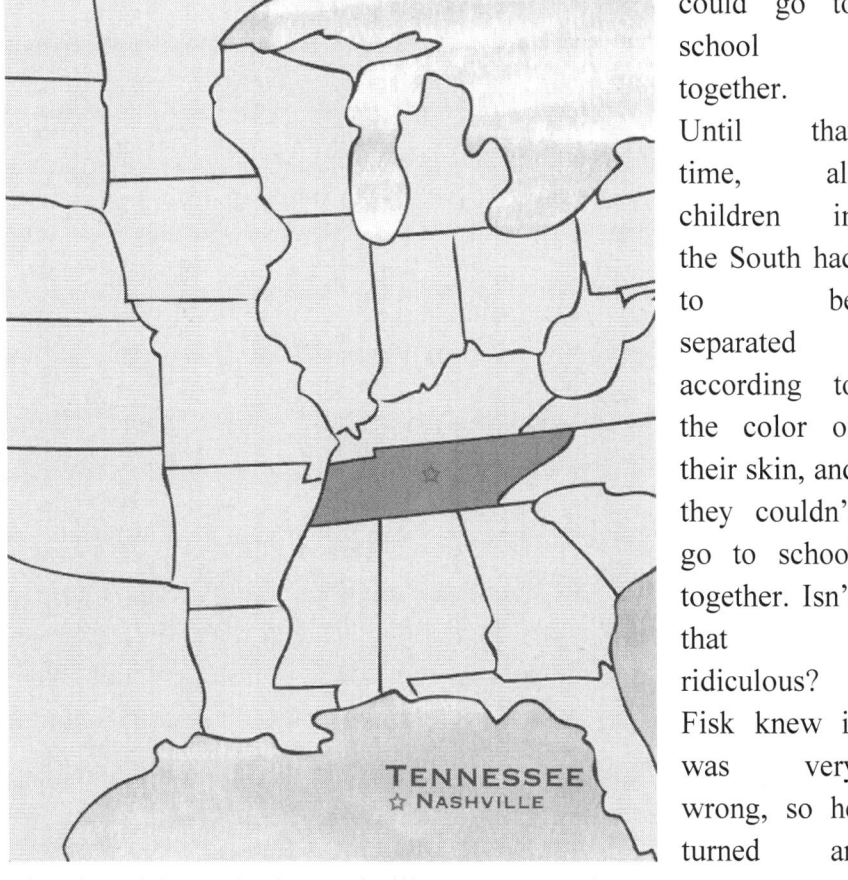

"In 1874, President Ulysses S. Grant appointed Fisk to the Board of Indian Commissioners. Fisk was very active in the temperance movement, which wanted to end drinking in America. They started their own political party called the Prohibition Party and selected Fisk to be their candidate to run for President of the United States in the 1888 election.

"It was an exciting race, with Ben Harrison running for the Republican Party against the sitting president Grover Cleveland, who was the candidate for the Democratic Party. All three men did their best to win the election, and Fisk came in third place. Benjamin Harrison won the election and became the President of the United States. I wonder what the world would be like today if he had won."

The big dog looked at the cats up in the tree, and he felt terrible. He knew that Fisk would not have been proud of him for trying to keep them out of the park.

Floppy said to him, "Why don't we act more like Fisk and invite our new friends to join us in the park?"

Bruno began to wag his tail. He liked that idea a lot. Patches and his friends liked that idea a lot too. They all spent the rest of the day lying in the soft grass together under the shade trees. Do you do your part to make sure that all people feel welcome everywhere you go? It shouldn't matter what a person looks like, whether they are short, tall, skinny, heavy, dark, light, have a disability, have an illness, are rich, poor, have an accent, are a different religion, have a different hair color, have a different style of clothes, or anything else. Make sure you're doing what you can to be like Fisk, Floppy, Bruno and Patches, and welcome everybody everywhere.

Bibliography:

"Clinton Fisk." *Wikipedia.* October 8, 2012.
<http://en.wikipedia.org/wiki/Clinton_Fisk>

The Importance of Dots and Dashes

History: Samuel Finley Breese Morse was born on April 27, 1791. He was an accomplished painter and sculptor, but he became most famous as a co-inventor of the telegraph and for developing Morse Code. He died on April 2, 1872 in New York City of

pneumonia. He was buried in Greenwood Cemetery in Brooklyn, New York. When he was inspired to invent an instant way to send messages across great distances, what resulted still makes our lives better today. Learning his story will make you realize what a great gift instant communication is to us all.

Jake was getting ready for his soccer game. He got dressed in his team uniform, found his cleats, and had his water bottle full. The only thing left to do was to find his shin guards.

Jake looked as hard as he could but couldn't find them anywhere. They weren't in the closet, under the bed, or even in the laundry basket. Where do you think Jake left them?

Mom said, "Come on Jake! If we don't leave now, you'll be late for the game!"

"But Mom, I can't find my shin guards anywhere! If I don't have them, I won't be able to play in the game!"

Mom said, "Where was the last place you had them?"

Jake thought and said, "I took them off in the car on the way home from practice."

Mom suddenly looked worried. She said, "Oh, no! Your Dad drove you home from practice! That means your shin guards are in his car, and we don't have them!" Has anything like that ever happened to you?

Jake was so upset that he didn't know what to do. This game was really important. If they won, they'd be in the championship playoffs. He just had to play!

To Jake's relief, Mom got her cell phone and sent Dad a text message. Dad messaged back right away and said he would meet them at the soccer field and bring Jake's shin guards.

"Whew! It's a good thing we have the ability to communicate instantly with people, no matter where they are!" Jake said gratefully.

He tried to imagine how difficult it would be to live in a time before we had cell phones and text messages, and he thought about Samuel Morse.

Samuel Morse was an artist who was born in Charlestown, Massachusetts on April 27, 1791. He loved to paint and sculpt and was so good at it that he became known for his ability to make portraits of people. Morse was hired to create portraits for many important political figures, including several presidents.

In 1825, Morse was in Washington D.C. working on a portrait. He received a letter that his wife was very ill. Morse left immediately, but, by the time he got home to New Haven, his wife had already died. It made him very sad, and he wished that there had been a way he could have known to come home sooner. It got his mind thinking about communication and how it could be made faster.

Several years later, in 1832, Morse was on a sea voyage aboard the ship *Sullyon* when he met a man named Charles Thomas Jackson, who studied electromagnetism. They talked about it, and Jackson showed Morse some of his experiments. Morse used his knew knowledge of electromagnetism to develop a single-wire telegraph.

Morse had to develop a code to use with his telegraph, made of dots and dashes that came to be called Morse Code. It is still used today and was the foundation for certain aspects of computer programming. What do you think he would say if he could see the technology we have today?

In 1837, Morse teamed up with two partners, Leonard Gale and Alfred Vail. They got a patent for their invention of the telegraph, and Morse set aside painting to work on developing it full time.

Believe it or not, Morse had a hard time convincing people that

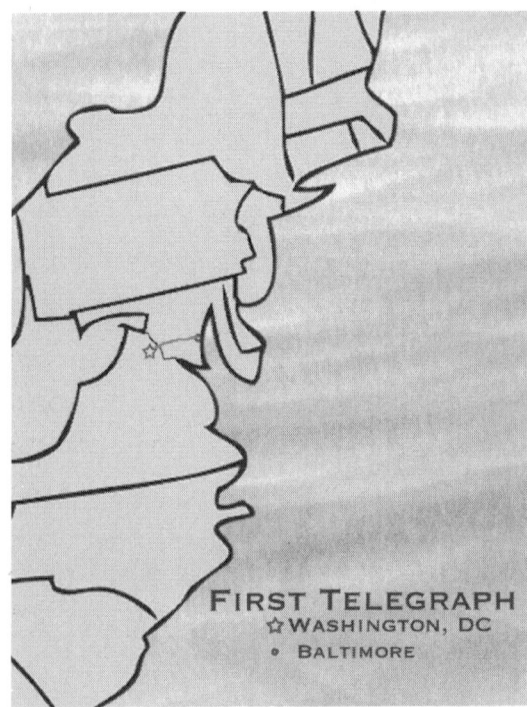

FIRST TELEGRAPH
☆ WASHINGTON, DC
• BALTIMORE

his invention was a good one. No one wanted to invest in it, and he was turned down by businessmen and skeptics everywhere. In 1843, Morse finally made a deal with Congress for the funds to build the first telegraph line from Baltimore to Washington D.C. By May of the following year, it was ready for use, and Morse got to send the first message by telegraph from the Capitol building in Washington all the way to Baltimore. He quoted the Bible and sent, "What hath God wrought."

Can you imagine how exciting that must have been? What message do you think you would have sent on such an important occasion?

The telegraph became a huge success with lines reaching across the country. It allowed messages to be sent almost instantly across great distances. Morse became very rich as a result and was very generous with his money. He made donations to artists, colleges, and many charities.

He died in New York City on April 2, 1872, just weeks before his 81st birthday. His invention still benefits us all today, as a foundation for computer networking and programming.

Jake stopped thinking of Morse as his mom pulled up in front of the soccer field and parked the car. He could see his Dad standing on the sidelines with his shin guards in his hands.

"Thanks Dad!" Jake said, as he ran up and gave his dad a hug before grabbing the shin guards and strapping them on his legs.

"No problem, buddy!" Dad said. "I'm just glad Mom was able to send me a message, or I wouldn't have known I even had them."

Have you ever had a time when you were grateful that you could communicate with someone instantly? Imagine what it would have been like if Morse had never invented the telegraph and we still lived in a time when messages could only be delivered by hand. Jake would have had to sit out the big game! The next time you communicate with someone instantly, whether it's by phone, text, or computer, think of Morse and know what a great world we live in because of inventors like him.

Bibliography:

"Samuel F. B. Morse." *United States History*. October 9, 2012. <www.u-s-history.com/pages/h1798.html>

"Samuel Morse." *Wikipedia*. October 9, 2012. <http://en.wikipedia.org/wiki/Samuel_Morse>

Great Grandma Steamboat

History: Steamboats shaped American history and culture when they were developed in the early 1800s to help traders navigate up the great rivers of the United States, including the Mississippi River, Ohio River, and Tennessee River. Steamboats were edged out by diesel boats in the 1920s. To see one still in action today,

look for the Delta Queen, Bell of Louisville, Natchez, Julia Bell Swain, Minnie Ha-ha, Chautauqua Bell, and the American Queen, among others. Seeing them in action is a beautiful way to remember our heritage. Hear the story of one steamboat to remember your own heritage and cherish just how special it is.

This is the mighty Mississippi River. Isn't it amazing? It starts at Itasca Lake in Minnesota and winds its way down the length of America. It divides the east part of the country from the west, and it forms the boundary of ten states. How many of them can you name?

Traders needed to find a way to travel upward against the strong currents of the river if the country was going to prosper, but how could anybody find an easy way to transport people and goods upriver?

That's where I come in! I'm a steamboat! I've got an engine that uses steam to power my paddle wheel. It allows me to travel upriver against the current with easy efficiency, even in shallow water! I've been used to transport cotton, timber, and even people. Steamboats like me were an important part of American history and the growth of trade.

My great-grandmother was a boat named *The New Orleans*. She was the first steamboat used on the Mississippi River and was launched in 1811 from Pittsburgh, Pennsylvania. Can you name your great-grandparents? Knowing your family history is important. It lets you know where you come from and how you got to be where you are today.

As more steamboats were built, trade grew quickly between Pittsburg and New Orleans, and soon even more boats were needed. In the 1810s, there were 20 steamboats on the river, but by the 1830s there were approximately 1,200!

Most steamboats were between 80 to 140 feet long and were 10 to 20 feet wide. Were your ancestors tall or short?

The boats were built almost entirely out of wood with iron trusses. The paddle wheel could be placed on the side of the boat or at the stern in the back. The boiler stack was placed in the center towards the front to give the boat balance. They burned wood or coal to create steam, which powered the engine and turned the paddles. What features did you inherit from your ancestors? What about the color of your hair or the shape of your nose? How about a love of animals or being left handed?

In my grandma's day, it took about three weeks for a steamboat to travel up the Mississippi River to the Ohio River. Over time, engines became more powerful and boat pilots gained more experience in knowing the waters. Soon, that trip could be made in as little as four days! Now that's travelling fast!

It could be a dangerous job navigating the Mississippi River, especially at such speeds! Ships could hit sand bars, snags, or each other! Sometimes they could catch fire from their boilers or just split apart at the hull from being poorly maintained. I bet your grandparents have some exciting tales to tell too.

In 1824, Congress passed the "Act to Improve the Navigation of the Ohio and Mississippi Rivers." As a result, the Army Corps of Engineers built canals to make passage safer where rapids made the river too dangerous to pass through.

Many American cities grew to be major trade centers because of steamboat traffic, including St Louis, Memphis, and New Orleans. Many famous stories involve steamboats as well, including works by the famous author Mark Twain, who wrote *Adventures of Huckleberry Finn,* among others. Have you ever read a book about steamboats or olden times?

As steamboat trade got busier, things got more dangerous. People got in such a hurry to make money with their steamboats that they failed to build them safely, and the boilers would explode. It is estimated that 4,000 people may have died from boiler explosions.

Finally, the government had enough and passed the "Steamboat Act of May 30, 1852." It allowed for the formation of an inspection process, which would ensure that boilers were built safely. From that point on, passengers could be assured their boat wouldn't explode from a poorly built boiler. Can you think of things that used to be dangerous, but have now been made safe?

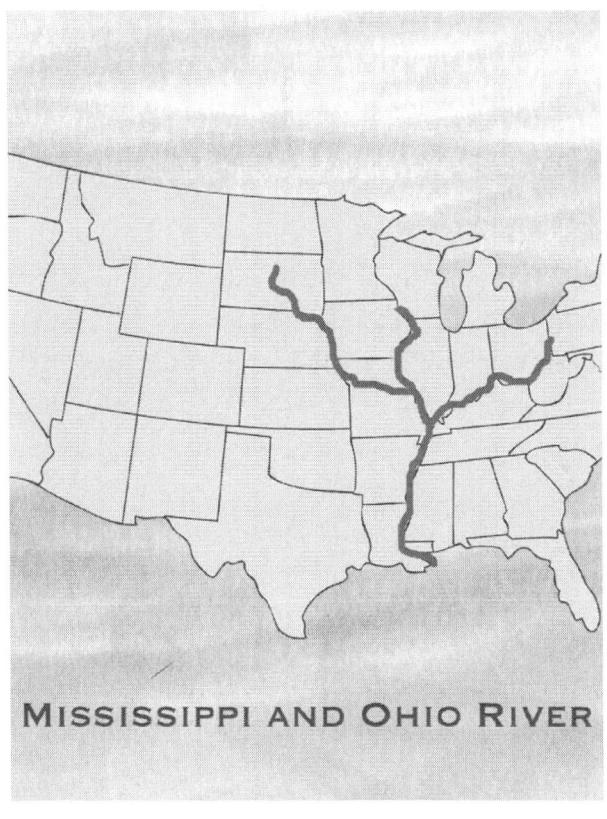

MISSISSIPPI AND OHIO RIVER

Being a passenger on a steamboat can be a lot fun. Many steamboats have been turned into museums or tourist attractions, and there are a few that are still paddling along the waters that people can ride on.

I love to talk with my grandmother about what it was like to be a steamboat paddling to St. Louis with a cargo hold full of molasses. She has some great stories about the time she almost hit a sandbar. She swerved to miss it and came within inches of colliding with another boat coming in the other direction. She said her life flashed in front of her hull!

I bet your grandparents have some stories that are even more interesting than hers! Sit down with your family one day and ask them to share with you some of the things that have happened to them. You can talk to aunts, uncles, cousins, or even your parents.

Ask them what it was like when they went to school. What kind of chores did they have to do? What was their first job? What was their favorite vacation? I bet there are a million questions you can think to ask.

Remember, when you know about your family's history, it tells you more about who you are and how you came to be where you are. I never would have known how lucky I am to be a steamboat with a safety valve on my steam stack and a side-wheel paddle if my grandmother hadn't taught me about her days on the Mississippi. Wait until you discover all the wonderful things you can learn too!

Bibliography:

"Steamboats of the Mississippi." *Wikipedia*. October 9, 2012. <http://en.wikipedia.org/wiki/Steamboats_of_the_Mississippi>

The Luckiest Kid on Earth

History: Henry Louis Gehrig lived from June 19, 1903 to June 2, 1941. He was a first baseman for the New York Yankees from 1923 to 1939, playing in 17 seasons and earning several major league records. He was stricken with ALS, and the disease has

come to be known by his name in his honor. He has been voted the greatest first baseman of all by the Baseball Writers Association.

Mark flopped down on the living room couch and sighed loudly.

"What's the matter, son?" his dad asked him.

"Everything!" Mark cried. "Nothing has been going right for me today. My favorite t-shirt was dirty, so I had to wear one I hate. We were all out of peanut butter and jelly, so I had to have ham for lunch instead. I stubbed my toe at recess. I have a history test on Friday, and now my favorite television show is a rerun!"

"That's a long list of disappointments." Dad sympathized.

"My whole life is ruined! Nothing goes the way I want it to!" Mark complained.

"I think you could use a little perspective," Dad said. "Let's go outside and play a little catch."

Dad handed Mark a baseball glove, grabbed a ball, and headed for the door.

Dragging his feet, Mark followed slowly behind. He asked, "What's perspective?"

"Perspective is how you view things," Dad explained. "Right now, you're looking at everything very negatively and seeing the worst of things. If you had a positive perspective, you could see the bright side of things."

They went out to the back yard, and Dad tossed the baseball at Mark. He tried to catch it in his mitt, but he dropped it and it fell to the ground. Mark said, "See! My life stinks! I can't even catch a ball!"

"It's a good thing Lou Gehrig didn't have your kind of negative attitude," Dad said. Mark tossed the ball to him, and he caught it with his glove and then tossed it back.

"Wasn't Lou Gehrig a baseball star?" Mark asked. He managed to catch the ball this time and tossed it back to his Dad.

"Not just any baseball star!" Dad said. "He was one of the greatest players who ever lived! He grew up in New York City. His parents had emigrated from Germany and weren't crazy about their son wanting to be a professional baseball player. Luckily, a talent scout disagreed. He saw Lou playing one day and offered him a sports scholarship to go to college.

"He went to Columbia University for two years. He didn't know it, but a scout for the Yankees, named Paul Krichell, was watching him during his college games. He was impressed by Lou's amazing talent. He was a great pitcher and set a team record when he struck out seventeen batters in a row. Even more impressive than that was the fact that he was left-handed hitting with a bat. Krichell had seen him hit a home run that went 450 feet! He knew he had to have him and, in 1923, signed him to play for the Yankees.

"Lou Gehrig's parents were poor, but they managed to scrape together the $14 their son needed to get to New Orleans for the spring training camp for the Yankees. For his first two seasons with the team, he didn't do much playing and mostly served as a pinch hitter.

"In 1926, the first baseman really came out of his shell, and after that he started giving the famous Babe Ruth real challenges for his records.

"Lou Gehrig was named the American League's Most Valuable Player twice. In 1932, he hit four home runs in a single game! He never missed a single game for 14 years and played in 2130 games! That set a record for the most consecutive games, which wasn't broken for fifty years. He also set a record for the most career grand slams – 23, a record which gained him the nickname 'The Iron Horse.'"

Mark and his dad continued to toss the baseball back and forth between each other. Mark said, "If I was as lucky as Lou Gehrig, I would have a positive attitude all the time too."

Dad said, "Ah, you think so, but his life wasn't always so lucky. At the end of the season in 1938, he started having trouble playing, and by 1939 it was clear that something was very wrong."

"What was it?" Mark asked with a worried frown.

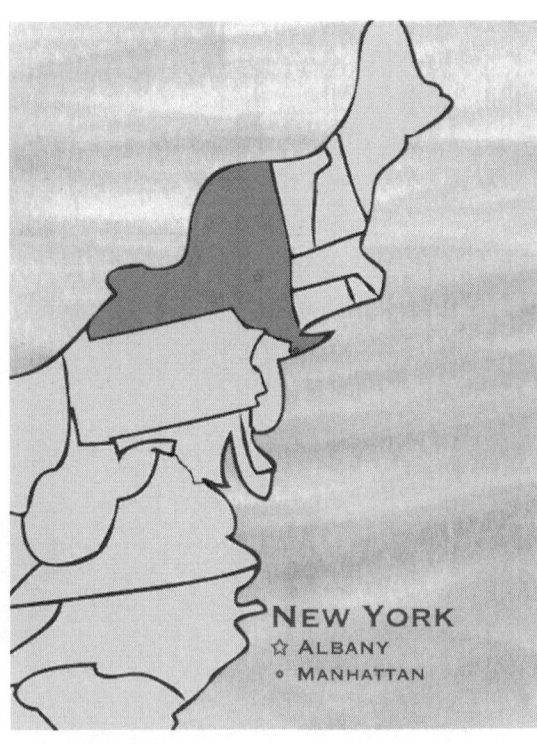

NEW YORK
☆ ALBANY
◦ MANHATTAN

"He went to the Mayo Clinic for testing, and on June 19, 1939 – his 36th birthday – he was diagnosed with ALS. That stands for amyotrophic lateral sclerosis, which is a disease that attacks the nervous system. It would make him paralyzed and unable to speak. The doctors said that he had less than three years left to live."

"Wow, and to think I was complaining about silly things like what t-shirt I had to wear and what television show I wanted to watch," Mark said. "I see what you mean about having the right perspective. With news like that, Lou Gehrig must have been really unhappy."

"Well, he knew he couldn't play baseball anymore, so he had to quit the Yankees. His teammates wanted to honor him with a special day at Yankee stadium on July 4, 1939. He gave a speech and said that he felt like 'the luckiest man on the face of the earth' because he'd been able to play professional baseball for so many years."

"Wow! If he felt so lucky after getting a deadly disease, I should feel really lucky for all the good things in my life! I'm healthy, have lots of clothes and toys, and plenty of food to eat. I think that makes me the luckiest kid on earth!"

"That's an attitude that would make heroes like Lou Gehrig proud," Dad smiled. "In 1939, he was voted into the Hall of Fame. He died on June 2, 1941 when he was only 37 years old. Everyone who knew him had nothing but great things to say about him, and ALS has become known as 'Lou Gehrig's Disease' in his honor."

"I'm sorry I had such a grumpy attitude before," Mark said to his Dad. "From now on, I'm going to look at things from the bright side – just like Lou Gehrig did."

Bibliography:

"Lou Gehrig." *Wikipedia*. October 10, 2012.
<http://en.wikipedia.org/wiki/Lou_gehrig>

"Lou Gehrig." *Garden of Praise*. October 10, 2012.
<http://www.gardenofpraise.com/ibdgehri.htm>

Dolley Madison

History: Dolley Payne Todd Madison was born on May 20, 1768 in Guilford County, North Carolina. She was the First Lady of the United States from 1809 to 1817 and known for her social grace, which has defined the role of the First Lady even today. She

died on July 12, 1849. She was originally buried in the Congressional Cemetery in Washington, D.C. but later re-interred at Montpelier estate in Virginia. We can learn a lesson from her on social grace and manners.

Zachary pulled at the collar of his shirt. He said, "Mom, why do I have to wear these fancy clothes? They're so uncomfortable!"

His mother smiled gently and adjusted his collar so his shirt didn't feel so tight around his neck, but Zachary still wasn't happy. He said, "Why do have to go to this boring party? Why can't we stay home and have fun?"

Mom said, "This party is being held by your Dad's boss. It's important for adults to go to these types of parties so they can have good relations with the people they work with."

"Will there be good food there and other kids to play with?" Zachary wanted to know.

"I'm sure there will be, but you must be on your good behavior and use your best manners," Mom said. "No running or shouting, use your fork and napkin, and always say please and thank you."

Zachary sighed. "I thought parties were supposed to be fun. Why do I have to follow all those rules and use boring manners?"

Mom said, "When you're at a party, that's when manners become the most important of all."

"What do you mean?" Zachary was curious.

"For hundreds of years, social gatherings have been of great importance, and the way a person acted at a party could have big effects. President Thomas Jefferson understood that part of his duty, as our nation's leader was to host dinners and receptions for other leaders and politicians. In those days, a man's wife acted as hostess and supervised such things, but Jefferson was a widow, which meant that his wife had died.

"His good friend, James Madison, whom he made his Secretary of State, was married to a charming young woman named Dolley. She graciously agreed to help the President and attended many events at his side. She was charming and generous, and everybody who met her loved her. When Jefferson wanted to expand our nation into the Louisiana Territory, it was Dolley Madison who helped him raise the funds he needed to send explorers Lewis and Clark on their expedition.

"Some people wanted to say that Dolley Madison was helping President Thomas Jefferson because they were having an affair, but the people who knew her and met her didn't believe such tales. In 1812, she helped her husband, James Madison, become the fourth President of the United States. She was now officially the fourth First Lady of the United States of America.

"Can you imagine what it would be like to live in the White House and be responsible for hosting dinners with important leaders?

"To celebrate her husband's inauguration, Dolley Madison agreed to attend a dance and dinner being held by Captain Tom Tingey, commandant of the Washington Navy Yard. So, on March 4, 1809, the very first Inaugural Ball was held – a tradition that still goes on today. There were 400 guests that evening, including the ministers of France and Britain.

"Unlike any of her predecessors, Dolley Madison believed her role as First Lady was an important one and that she had a duty to use her status to benefit her country. She redecorated the White House to impress diplomats and always made every guest feel

106

relaxed and comfortable. She understood the importance of using parties and dinners to enhance relations and build alliances."

When Mom had finished telling her story, Zachery looked at her very thoughtfully. He frowned and said, "Are you saying that, when I use my manners at a party, I'm acting like the First Lady?"

"No!" Mom laughed lovingly. "I'm saying that, when you attend a party, you are acting like a diplomat for our family. The

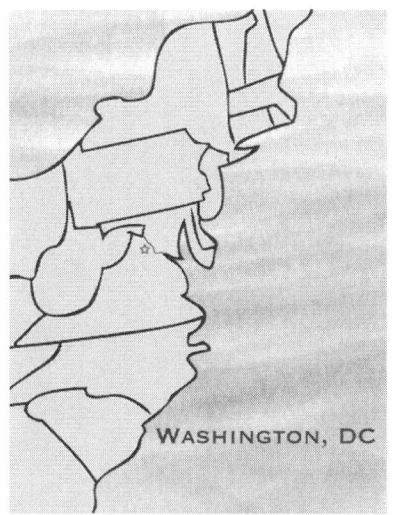

WASHINGTON, DC

way you act and behave at a party shows everybody there what kind of family we are. Are we a family who is polite and considerate? Are we a family who says please and thank you? Or are we a family who is rude, selfish, cuts in front of others, burps at the table, and shouts in the house?"

"I see!" Zachery smiled. "So I can think of every party I go to as a chance to show everybody how good our family is, just like Dolley Madison used every party to show how good the President and America was?"

"Exactly!" Mom smiled proudly. Do you remember to use your manners when you go to a party or out to dinner? Which manners do you think are the most important?

Bibliography:

"First Lady Biography: Dolley Madison." *National First Ladies Library*. October 13, 2012. <www.firstladies.org/biographies/firstladies.aspx?biography>

Let Freedom Ring

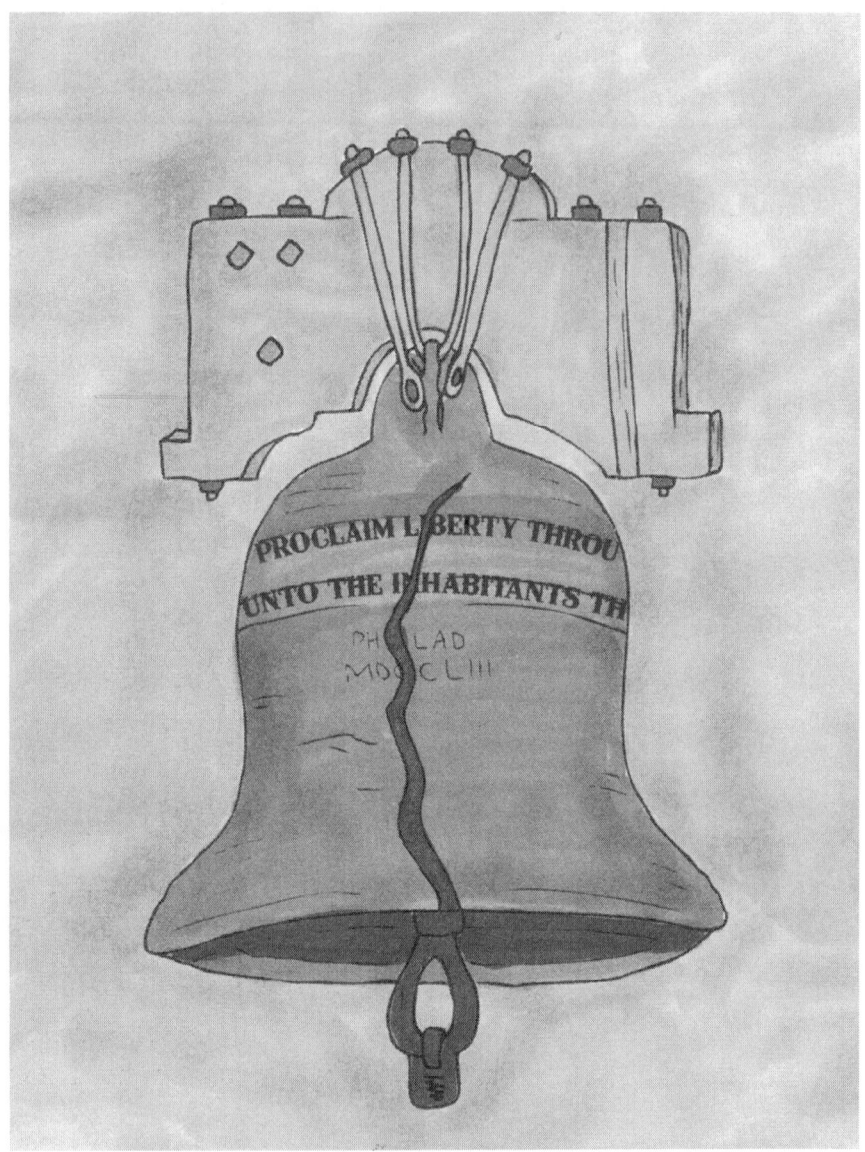

History: Originally cast in 1752, the Liberty Bell has become an iconic symbol of freedom. It weighs about 2000 pounds and is made of 70% copper, 25% tin, and small amounts of lead, arsenic, zinc, silver, and gold. It currently resides in the Independence

Visitor Center in Old City, Philadelphia in Pennsylvania. The Liberty Bell offers us the supreme example of the value of repairing and reusing broken items.

When I was little, back in 1751, I heard the town bell ringing. Mama called for me to come into the house. She said that, when the bell rang, it meant danger. Pa was out in the barn tending to the animals. He dropped everything and ran to see what the matter was.

It turned out to be a terrible fire. It burned most of the buildings in our town. After that, Pa couldn't earn enough money to make a living, and we had to move. He told Ma that we would go to the big city of Philadelphia. I had lived in our small country town all my life, so I was nervous about moving to such a big place. Have you ever had to move someplace that was different like that?

When we arrived in Philadelphia, I couldn't believe how huge it was! It would take an entire day to walk from one end of the city to the other! In the town I had come from, you could see everything there was to see in just a few hours. I felt lost in such a huge place.

There were so many people everywhere. Many of them had emigrated from other countries and spoke different languages. There were shops and businesses of every kind. But once I got over being scared, it was really very exciting.

Pa noticed that the city didn't have a clock tower with a bell in it, like most towns did. He said to Ma, "How do they ever know what time it is or when danger is coming?"

Pa wasn't the only one wondering that. I was playing one day when I heard the city leaders talking about it. They all felt it was important that they have a bell, but it couldn't just be any bell. It would need to be one that was big enough to be heard all across the huge city. They decided to order one all the way from London, England.

I had forgotten all about the conversation I had heard until a year later. It was the August of 1752 when a huge crate arrived from London. The whole city was excited to see the bell it contained. It looked absolutely perfect, but, when it was rung for the first time, it cracked at the rim. Everyone was horribly disappointed.

It would not be possible to send the bell all the way back to London. Two men by the name of John Pass and John Stow offered to recast the bell. Neither one of them was a professional bell maker, but they were smart men, and they thought the bell could work if only it were a little stronger.

Pass and Stow melted the bell down and added ten percent more copper to make it stronger. By March of 1753, it was ready to be tested. They had included their names in writing on it, but perhaps they shouldn't have.

Lots of people showed up to hear the ringing of the new bell. There were so many people crowded around me that I had to stand on a stack of crates to be able to see over their heads. Have you ever been to an event where you couldn't see over the crowd?

When the new bell was rung for the first time, it did not break, but the sound it made was terrible. Everyone in the crowd laughed, and many people mocked it.

I would have given up then and there. What would you have done?

Well, Pass and Stow weren't ready to give up yet. They melted the bell down again and recast it for the third time. Just a few months later, in June of 1753, they were ready to test the newest version of the bell.

A huge crowd came once more. This time, I couldn't even get a spot standing on top of the crates. I had to push my way to the front of the crowd and squeeze in between two men, who nearly crushed me. We all held our breath as they rang the bell, hoping it would be all right.

To the immense joy of all, the bell rang loud and clear. Its tone was good, and it did not crack! Pass and Stow had done it! The bell was hung in the steeple of the Pennsylvania State House. I was glad that Pass and Stow hadn't given in to defeat and that they kept trying – so were a lot of other people. Whenever there was an important public meeting being held, a proclamation being read, or lawmakers needed to be called to session, the bell would be rung for all to hear.

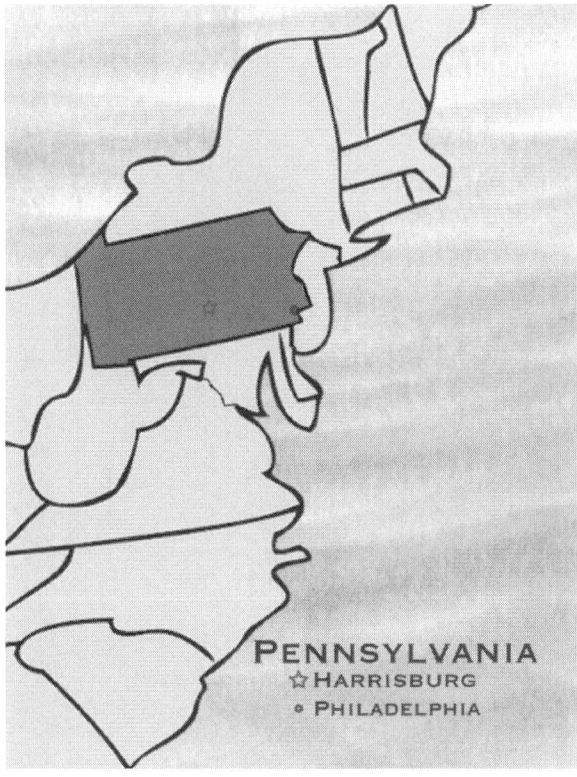

When I grew up, I got married and moved away from Philadelphia. My wife and I had many children and even more grandchildren. One day, I decided to take a trip to Philadelphia with my granddaughter, Sophia, to show her where I had gone to school.

When we strolled past the bell tower, I saw that the mighty bell had, at last, developed a huge crack. I asked a man passing by, "When did that happen?"

He said that the rumor was it had cracked when it was rung after the death of a popular judge, Chief Justice John Marshall, in 1835. I do not know if that rumor was true or whether it was just a story. All I know for sure is that, over time, the bell has grown to become a symbol of liberty, freedom, and the American way of life. Thus, people have come to call it the Liberty Bell, as these fine words were written on it: "Proclaim liberty throughout all the land unto all the inhabitants thereof."

Have you ever made something that didn't turn out right? Have you ever taken something that was broken and been able to fix it and keep using it? The Liberty Bell is a symbol of freedom, but it also shows that, just because something doesn't come out right the first time or breaks, it can still have value. When you find something that has broken, don't just throw it out right away. Consider if there is a way to repair or reuse it first. We wouldn't have the Liberty Bell today if Pass and Stow hadn't done just that same thing.

Bibliography:

"Liberty Bell Center." *National Park Service*. October 12, 2012. <www.nps.gov/inde/liberty-bell-center.htm>

"Liberty Bell." *Wikipedia*. October 12, 2012. <www.nps.gov/inde/liberty-bell-center.htm>

Fort Caroline

History: Fort Caroline was the first French Colony established in the present-day United States, in what is now Jacksonville, Florida. It began when Jean Ribault left some men and tried to start a colony between Bluffton S.C. and Charleston, after an expedition in February 1562 landed near the present day Fort Caroline in northern Florida. The goal was to form a settlement for France. The leaders were all Huguenots. The fort at Fort Caroline was subsequently established by René Laudonniere on June 22, 1564. The colony was short-lived, as it was destroyed by the Spanish in 1565. The site is now called Fort Caroline National Memorial and is a unit of the Timucuan Ecological and Historic Preserve. Read this story and learn what important role singing

played in Fort Caroline, and also what important role it can play in your own life too.

Brandon dragged his feet unhappily. He hated going to music practice. It's not that he hated music. In fact he loved music and was always listening to the radio and singing along to his favorite songs. He just hated having to sing the same boring songs they always sang at practice. They were so old, that his grandfather said, they were the same songs he used to sing as a boy. Do you know any songs that your parents or grandparents used to sing?

"Why do we have to sing these old songs?" Brandon complained to the teacher. "Why can't we sing new songs?"

Mrs. Peterson smiled kindly at Brandon. "I used to feel the same way, but then I discovered there is something very special about singing songs that everyone knows. One day, you'll be able to teach these songs to your children and your grandchildren. The songs are a great way that we can all stay connected to each other, generation after generation."

Brandon just shook his head. He didn't care what she said. He still hated singing those same boring old songs and didn't see any point. He couldn't wait for music practice to be over! As soon as it was done, he was leaving for a vacation to stay with his cousins. They lived far away, in another state!

Staying with his cousins was a lot of fun, but everything was different. They ate different food and played different games. Even though he was having fun, Brandon found himself feeling a little homesick. Have you ever felt homesick when you've stayed somewhere?

He went with his cousins to their music practice, but by then he was so sad all he wanted to do was sit by himself while the others sang. There was a shelf of books nearby, and he picked one up and started reading it. It was about a little bird. The story went like this:

114

The Mocking Bird, the official state bird of Florida, having a brown and white chest with black and white wings and a grey head, was sitting on an Orange Blossom, which is the official flower of the State of Florida. It was looking for insects and spiders to eat. The tasty bugs of the North Florida forests were its favorite food. Brandon stuck out his tongue and made a face. He couldn't imagine eating bugs, can you? Suddenly, the Mocking Bird heard the sound of people walking through the trees. The little brown bird thought about making his loud cry of "teakettle-teakettle-teakettle!" to scare them off, but he decided to hide and watch them instead. Brandon knew that's what he would have done too, how about you?

The people that the Mocking Bird saw were very strange! They did not look anything like the Timucuan Indians or people he was used to seeing. These were people from France, wearing strange clothes, some with vests that looked like shields and carrying weapons and supplies. It was the spring of 1562, and the people were a group of Huguenots, merchant marine sailors and Moors or black African sailors. Brandon knew that meant they were Protestants from France. They were being lead by a man named Jean Ribault. He had brought 150 Huguenots in three ships to the New World. They wanted to make a colony where they could live and worship their religion, which they were not allowed to do in France.

The little bird was curious about these strange people. They began to build a fort that they called Fort Caroline, in honor of their king Charles IX. While they worked, they liked to sing songs. Brandon smiled, because he liked to sing or listen to music when he had to do chores at home too. The songs the men were singing were unlike anything the bird had ever heard before. They were Psalms in Acapella. Do you know any songs in Acapella? La, la, la ....higher la,la la.

The Native Americans that lived in the forest of Northern Florida and Southern Georgia were curious about these strange people, just like the little bird was. Mr. Ribault was able to teach some of the Timucuan people how to sing Huguenot songs (1). They liked them and a friendship was formed. After a Monument was erected near Mayport Florida close to the beach, they traded goods and their ships sailed away north.

The Mocking Bird had a cousin in South Carolina near Hilton Head Island and Charleston. He had heard some chirping stories carried from a traveling flock of other birds that was overheard from white and black men in strange clothes. These men were floating on wood, traveling south of them a few hundred miles away, which for a bird, isn't that far. Can you imagine flying through the air seeing the spanish moss in the majestic oak trees, pine trees so straight and tall and all the tidal creeks that go up and down from high tide to low?

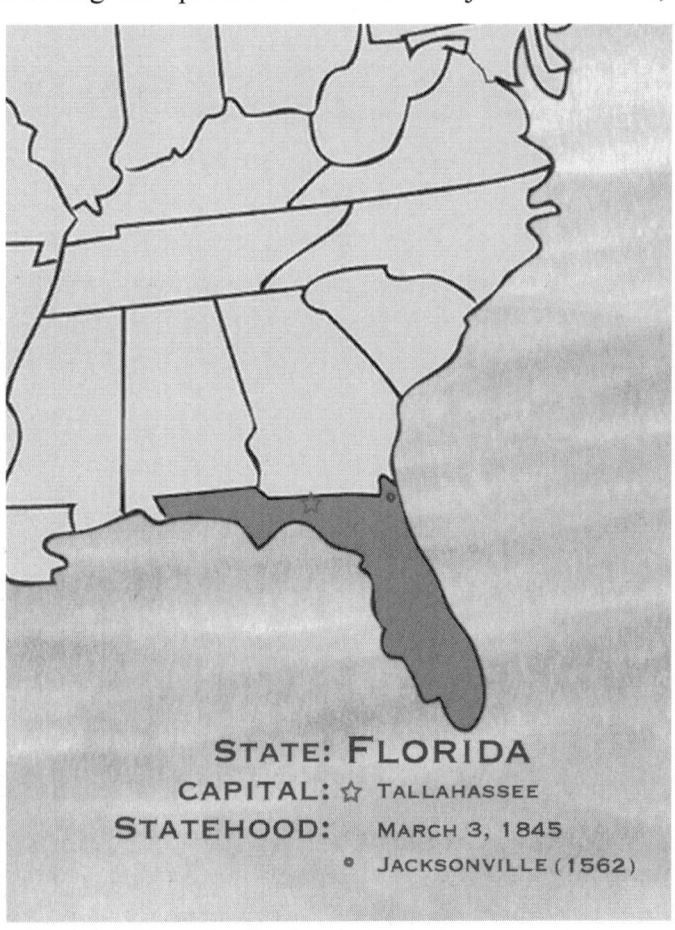

The Mocking Bird's cousin saw them come ashore from, the wooden floating device and look around. Next thing you know

STATE: FLORIDA

CAPITAL: ☆ TALLAHASSEE

STATEHOOD: MARCH 3, 1845

◦ JACKSONVILLE (1562)

116

they were cutting down some of the tall trees and building a people house, kind of like a bird house but on the ground. They hunted for wild animals and fished in the salt water. Then one day;

Mr. Ribault decided to sail back to France to get more supplies. So he left about two dozen men and went away on the wooden device. When he got there, he found that a religious conflict had broken out and he had to flee France. He went to Queen Elizabeth of England and asked for her help. She thought he was a spy and had him thrown in prison in the Tower of London.

The men at Charlesfort were desperate as they waited. Finally they built a boat and sailed away. Several years later, the king of France sent Mr. Ribault's lieutenant, who was named René Laudonniere, to go to Fort Caroline to help the struggling colonists. He took 304 people with him and stared a fort called Fort Caroline high on a bluff off the river May, which is now called the St Johns River. As Mr. Laudonniere searched for some of his old Indian friends in the new territory, he heard a familiar song and knew he was in the right place. Imagine his surprise when he discovered those same Psalms were being sung by the Timucuan's! Brandon smiled to himself, thinking how cool that would be! Have you ever heard a familiar song in a strange place?

Sharing the words to the familiar songs helped the colonists and the Timucuans know they were among friends and the colony at Fort Caroline was able to thrive for a time. When Mr. Ribault was finally released from the Tower of London in 1565, he quickly outfitted a few ships and return to Fort Caroline. Have you ever heard of your friends being somewhere ahead of you and how quickly you packed your things and wanted to get there?

Because of the gold in Mexico the Spanish did not want to allow the French to have a fort so close to the Gulf Stream. The Gulf Stream is a current of water, with lots of fish and other marine life, that flows from the Gulf of Mexico, around the Florida Keys and within 60 miles of Jacksonville or Ft Caroline. A Spanish admiral by the name of Pedro Menendez was sent to stop the French and started a fort in St. Augustine called Castillo de San Marcos. So Mr. Menendez invaded the colony and stopped them. Sadly Mr. Ribault was killed, but Mr. Laudonniere survived to tell Mr. Ribault's brothers in France the amazing story. Mr. Ribault's relatives came all the way back across the Atlantic ocean to Huguenot Park near Talbot Island in North Florida. They recognized Indians of the Timucuan tribe singing their songs they had learned from Mr. Ribault. Knowing that they were close, they sneaked up and re-took Fort Caroline, and then went back home to France

Brandon closed the book about Fort Caroline and smiled to himself. Just then his cousin's music practice began. They were singing one of the songs he always sang at his music class at home! Brandon found his lips moving to the words, and soon he was singing along with them. It made him feel a lot less homesick to sing the familiar song, and before he knew it, he was happy and having fun. Brandon didn't even notice that he wasn't homesick anymore as he sang song after song.

When his vacation with his cousins was over, Brandon returned home. He couldn't wait to go to his music practice and tell Mrs. Peterson that they sang the same songs where his cousins lived and how fun it was to able to sing together with them, and already know the words.

Mrs. Peterson and Ribault both already knew what Brandon had just learned. There is great power of communication and friendship in sharing the words of a song. What songs do you know that are shared songs like that? Do your parents and grandparents know them? What many places can you go where people know that same song? Do you think one day you will teach that song to your own children? If you do, then you will be part of the chain of friendship and love that began with the first person to share that song, which is a great thing.

Bibliography:

United States History, Jean Ribault, viewed November 24, 2012 at
http://www.u-s-history.com/pages/h1147.html

Wikipedia, Fort Caroline, viewed November 24, 2012 at
http://en.wikipedia.org/wiki/Fort_Caroline

One (1) - Arise America is a musical album containing these songs that were taught to the Timucuan Indians. These original songs were discovered by Mickey Roman. After adding timing to the music he was able to record it and publish it. Arise America can be found online on www.arisepublishing.com

How to Spell Greatness

History: Noah Webster was born in Hartford, Connecticut on October 16, 1758. He sought to create a foundation for nationalism through education. The textbooks he created have taught generations of children how to spell, and his name has become

synonymous with the word "dictionary." He had eight children with his wife Rebecca and died at the age of 84 on May 28, 1843. He is buried in Grove Street Cemetery in New Haven, Connecticut. Read his story to learn how this great man has influenced a nation.

"Look at him go!" said the little gray mouse, Peter, as he watched the school teacher.

"What's he doing now?" asked the little brown mouse, Polly.

"He's climbing a ladder to patch the roof!" Peter exclaimed.

"I don't know why he bothers." Polly shook her furry head. "That school house is nothing better than a shack. Not only does that school teacher have to clean the building, but he has to do all the repairs on it himself – and boy does it need a lot!"

"Yeah, but just look at the way he cares about the students," said Peter, hugging his tail. "You can see that he really cares for them and wants them to have the best education."

Polly saw that Peter was right. The young school teacher, Noah Webster, was a good man, teaching all those students in a little shack in Connecticut. Eventually, he became a schoolmaster in Hartford and studied law. He became a lawyer, but his passion laid in teaching, and he decided to write a book about spelling and grammar.

"Where's he going now?" Polly asked, as Webster climbed onto his horse.

"He's traveling from one town to the next, across the 13 colonies," Peter said, brushing his whiskers.

"What for?" asked Polly. She couldn't understand why that man still worked so hard. He could just sit back and be a wealthy lawyer if he wanted to, but he didn't.

His spelling book was called *American Books for American Children*, and he could convince a school to buy hundreds at a time for all their students. He ended up selling more than 100 million copies, and the book grew to be known as the *Blue-backed Speller*.

"What's he doing now?" Polly asked impatiently. She was sure that Webster would sit back on his fortune now, but instead he was working even harder than before.

"He's trying to help develop a 'mother tongue,'" Peter said.

"What does that mean?" Polly asked. Do you know the answer?

Peter answered, saying, "People have come here to America from many different countries, and they have a hard time communicating sometimes. Mr. Webster thinks that he could make it easier for people to understand each other by having them all speak one language, called a 'mother tongue.' He's making a dictionary that will explain what all the words mean and how to pronounce them."

"That sounds like a lot of work!" Polly said.

"It is, but when he's done it will be well worth the effort. It will unite all Americans under one language and allow them to communicate and understand each other better."

The two little mice were right. It took Noah Webster more than 20 years and thousands of dollars to create his dictionary. He researched the origins and meanings of words by going to libraries in England, France, and the United States. When he was done, he had created a dictionary of 70,000 words, and he'd done it all by himself. He called it *An American Dictionary of the English*

Language. His book has sold more copies of any other English book, except for the Bible.

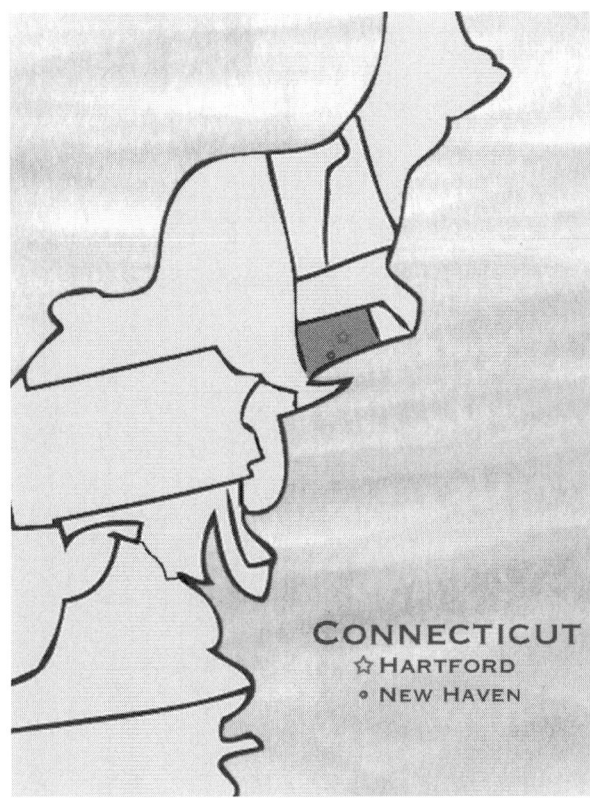

CONNECTICUT
☆ HARTFORD
◦ NEW HAVEN

Noah Webster's dictionary helped change America and unite us all to be able to talk with each other and understand each other. Imagine what life would be like if everybody still spoke the language of their ancestors and we had no common language to use at businesses, schools, and with our friends.

"What's going on now?" Polly asked.

"Quiet! I can't hear what the next word is!" Peter shushed. The two little mice were hiding in the wall of the gymnasium at Webster Elementary School.

"I want to know what all those kids are doing lined up in there!" Polly insisted.

"They're participating in a spelling bee," Peter said, holding his paw up to his ears, trying to hear better.

"What's a spelling bee?" Polly asked.

"It's a contest, in which students are given words to spell. If they spell the word correctly, they get to stay in the competition, but, if they make a mistake, they are out. When only one speller is left, that person is declared the winner of the spelling bee."

"I bet Noah Webster would be proud to see that Americans are taking their spelling so seriously," Polly said.

"I think you're right!" Peter smiled. What do you think?

"Hey, where are you going?" Peter asked Polly, as he saw her scampering away.

"I'm going to go study my spelling words for the test I have on Friday! I never realized what a great thing it was to be able to spell, but, now that I know, I'm going to always give spelling my best effort!"

Peter smiled. "Now I bet Noah Webster would be proud of you too!"

Bibliography:

"Noah Webster." *Famous Leaders for Young Readers, Garden of Praise*. October 12, 2012. <http://www.gardenofpraise.com/ibdnoahw.htm>

"Noah Webster." *Wikipedia*. October 12, 2012. <http://en.wikipedia.org/wiki/Noah¬Webster>

The Unsinkable Molly Brown

History: Margaret Tobin Brown was born on July 18, 1867 in Hannibal, Missouri. She was a philanthropist and suffragette who gained famed by surviving the sinking of the Titanic. She died on October 26, 1932 at the age of 65 in New York City. Her story

about bravely fighting for what is right teaches us all to do the same.

Ashley was playing on the swing set at school during recess. It was her favorite activity. She loved the feel of the wind on her face and her hair flowing behind her as she soared through the air. She pumped her legs hard, driving herself to swing higher and higher.

From way up high, Ashley could see the whole playground. She could see Tommy and Jose playing handball against the south wall. She could see Jennifer and Anna playing hopscotch by the basketball hoops. She could see Max and Sophia climbing on the jungle gym. What's your favorite thing to do on the playground?

Suddenly, Ashley noticed something strange. Three older boys were standing by the water fountain, blocking it. A young boy from a lower grade went to the fountain to get a drink. The three older boys surrounded him and started to push him. Ashley realized that the little boy was being bullied.

Ashley felt very scared. She knew that she was witnessing something that was wrong. The three bullies needed to be stopped, but what could she do? She was just one girl. She didn't have the power to stop three bullies, or did she?

Ashley thought about Molly Brown. She was just one woman living around the turn of the century, but she had been able to accomplish great things.

Molly had been born Margaret Tobin on July 18, 1867 in Hannibal Missouri. She married a man named James Joseph Brown, whom everybody called J.J., when she was just eighteen years old.

They were both relatively poor until J.J. suddenly became very wealthy when the mine where he worked struck ore. Molly wanted to use their money to help others. She became involved in women's suffrage, trying to get women the right to vote. She worked in soup kitchens to feed the poor. Wherever she saw a need, Molly Brown tried to do what she could to help.

Molly gained great fame by surviving the sinking of the Titanic and came to be called "The Unsinkable Molly Brown." The Titanic sank on April 15, 1912 after hitting an iceberg. There were not enough lifeboats for all the passengers. Molly was placed in Lifeboat 6, and it broke her heart to see all the people suffering in the freezing cold water after the ship went down. She knew that they would die if no one came to rescue them.

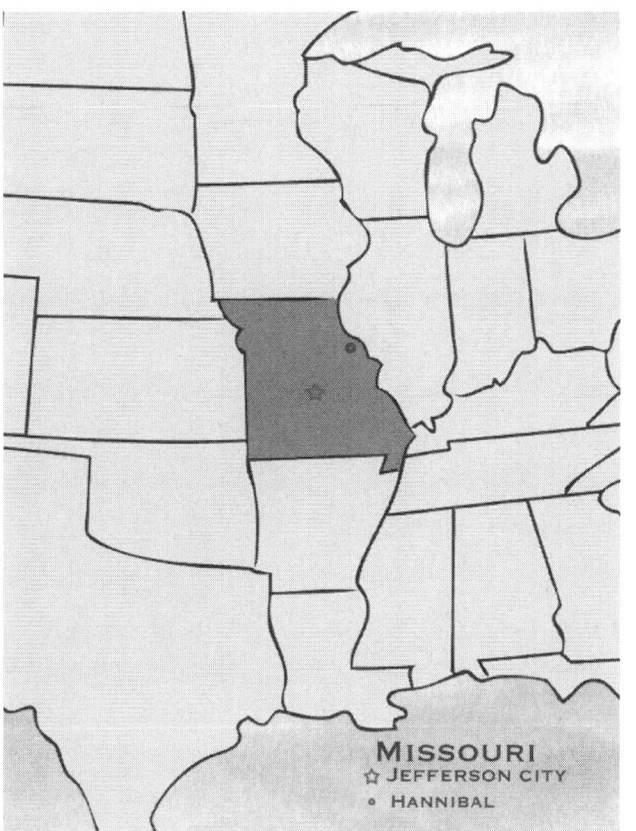

MISSOURI
☆ JEFFERSON CITY
• HANNIBAL

The Quartermaster, Robert Hichens, was in charge of her lifeboat. He did not want to go back and rescue any of the people suffering in the water. He feared that, if he did, they would swarm the lifeboat and they would all die too. Molly Brown didn't care. She knew that helping those people in the water was the right thing to do. She argued with the Quartermaster until she convinced him to go back.

Ashley realized that Molly Brown was right; doing the right thing is always the right thing to do. She had to do something to stop those bullies from pushing that young boy. Ashley looked around the playground and saw a teacher, Mrs. Bennett, standing by the jungle gym. Ashley stopped her swing and ran to her. She told Mrs. Bennett that she had witnessed someone being bullied. Mrs. Bennett rushed to put an end to it. The three bullies were sent home from school, and the principal himself thanked Ashley for her bravery in doing what was right.

When you see something wrong happening, find a safe adult and let them know. It's always the right thing to do.

Bibliography:

"Margaret Brown." *Wikipedia.* October 13, 2012. <http://en.wikipedia.org/wiki/Molly_Brown>

Susan B. Anthony

History: Susan B. Anthony was born on February 15, 1820 in Adams, Massachusetts. She was a leader in the Women's Rights movement of the 19th century, fighting for Women's Suffrage by giving countless speeches. She died on March 13, 1906 at the age

of 86 in Rochester, New York. Her story reminds us all not to take our right to vote for granted and to cherish it and use it.

When I grow up, I am going to vote! I can hardly wait until I turn eighteen, so I can cast my first ballot. I'll be able to have a voice in our government. Are you going to vote when you grow up too?

Some people choose not to vote. They think it's too much trouble, or they don't feel like deciding who to vote for. Our ancestors had to work really hard to give us the right to vote. I think, if more people knew what they had to go through, they would realize what a big deal voting was.

Sure, a lot of people know about the Revolutionary War, when we won our independence from England, but that didn't give everybody the right to vote. In 1850, white men had enjoyed the right to vote for years, and black men had gained the right the vote with the fourteenth amendment, but women still could not vote.

Can you imagine that? None of the women in our entire country could vote! It sounds crazy today, but, back then, people thought that was the way it should be. Well, not all people.

A woman named Susan B. Anthony didn't think it should be that way at all. How about you?

Susan was very smart, and she cared about a lot of things. She was against slavery, against drinking, and wanted women to have fair treatment in society. She wanted women to have equal pay, the right to own property, and the right to vote. In her time, women didn't have any of those things. She became a powerful speaker and published a weekly journal called *The Revolution.*

In 1872, after the Fourteenth Amendment had passed, guaranteeing all people had the right to vote, Susan went to the office of voter registration and asked to register. She found more women and got them to register too. They voted in that year's presidential election on November 5, 1872, and Ulysses S. Grant became the president of the U.S.

Two weeks later, a deputy marshal came and arrested Susan for having voted. All the other women who had voted in the election were arrested too. People heard about it, and it gave her an opportunity to spread her message. She gave speeches all over Monroe County where she lived, asking people to consider how unfair it was that any person could be denied the right to vote.

NEW YORK
☆ ALBANY
• MONROE COUNTY

Her trial was held in New York before Supreme Court Associate Justice Ward Hunt. He refused to let her testify on her own behalf and found her guilty without allowing her to have trial by jury. She was given a fine of $100. Do you think that was fair?

Susan B. Anthony continued to campaign for women's rights, although she did not live to see the day when her dream came true. She died on March 13, 1906. Fourteen years after her death, women were finally granted the right to vote on August 26, 1920 by the Nineteenth Amendment to the Constitution.

That is why, when I grow up, I am going to vote in every election. I'm not going to say that I am too busy or just don't know who to vote for. I'm going to take my right to vote seriously and use it to have my voice in government. How about you?

Bibliography:

"Biography." *National Susan B. Anthony Museum and House*. October 12, 2012. <http://susanbanthonyhouse.org/her-story/biography.php>

"Susan B. Anthony." *Wikipedia*. October 12, 2012. <http://en.wikipedia.org/wiki/Susan_b_anthony>

House of History

History: The White House is the official residence of the President of the United States. In 1792, George Washington commissioned James Hogan to design and build it. President John Adams became the first to live there, when he moved in November

1800, and every U.S. President has lived there since. Learn why the White House is proud to be a part of American history and why you should have pride in the home where you live too.

Hello. Can you guess who I am? I am a famous building that was designed by a man named James Hoban. He made me in the neoclassical style, and I was built between 1792 and 1800. My picture is on the back of the twenty dollar bill.

Still not sure? I'll give you another clue – you can find me at 1600 Pennsylvania Avenue Northwest, Washington D.C. I've had the special privilege of being the home to every U.S. President since John Adams! I bet you can guess who I am now!

That's right! I'm the White House! I contain the residence and offices of the President of the United States of America.

I didn't always look the way I do today. I started out pretty small and just kept growing to fit the needs of the presidency. It began when Thomas Jefferson created two colonnades for me in 1801 that were designed to hide my stables and storage area.

Then, in 1814, something terrible happened. The British Army attacked Washington D.C. and set me on fire, in what came to be called the "Burning of Washington." My interior was completely destroyed, and my exterior was badly charred. They began to rebuild me right away, and, in October 1817, I was repaired enough for President James Monroe to take residence again. I felt really proud that he moved back in, even though my reconstruction wasn't fully complete yet. It showed me how much I meant to the presidency and the country.

In 1824, I grew bigger when a South Portico was added and even bigger still with a North Portico in 1829. Even with all those colonnades and porticos, things were crowded, so in 1901 President

Theodore Roosevelt had all work offices moved into my newly constructed West Wing. About eight years later, President William Howard Taft expanded the West Wing with the creation of the Oval Office.

I didn't just keep growing wider; I also grew taller, when my attic was turned into a third floor for living quarters in 1927. Today, I have six stories, including a ground floor, state floor, second floor, third floor, and a two story basement. I have 132 rooms, 35 bathrooms, 28 fire places, 8 staircases, and 3 elevators. My total floor space equals 55,000 ft². I also have a bowling alley, movie theater, tennis court, jogging track, swimming pool, and putting green.

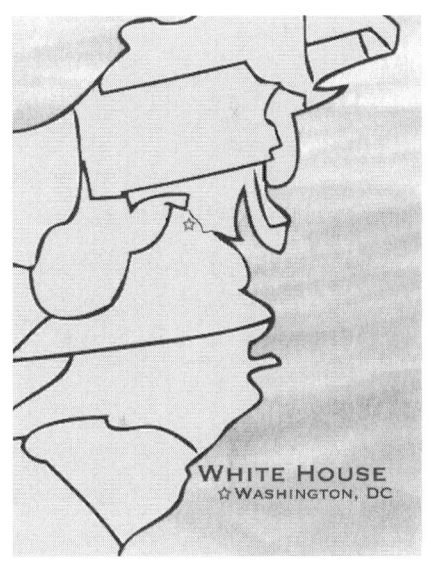

It's never lonely being the White House. Every week, approximately 30,000 visitors come to tour me. It's lots of fun because I get to show off my rainbow of rooms. I have rooms named after lots of colors, including the Green Room, Blue Room, Red Room, and Yellow Room. Each room is decorated in the color that it is named after and used for important functions, like entertaining leaders from other countries. I also have a China Room, which is filled with the china dishes of previous presidents, a Map Room, and a Library.

Of course, I'm still a house where the President lives with his family, so I have the types of rooms any regular house would have too, including a kitchen, family room, dining room, and bedrooms, except mine are probably much bigger and fancier than most.

Now, I'm not just a house, I also happen to be an office, where the president and many government employees work every day. All of that takes place in my West Wing. I have a room where the President can meet with his Cabinet of advisors and a room where the Press can come and get important information. What kind of rooms does your house have?

Outside, I have a beautiful rose garden and many trees. Several of my magnolia trees have been growing here since they were planted by Andrew Jackson. First Lady Michelle Obama planted my first organic vegetable garden and installed beehives to produce honey. It makes me feel proud to know that I am growing the food being fed to the First Family and their many important guests.

Have you ever grown a vegetable garden? You don't have to have a big house like me in order to have a garden. You don't even have to have a yard. You can grow plants in containers that you set in your window or on your patio. Lots of people grow gardens in containers that they set outside the window of their apartment in the city.

I hope that one day you can come and visit me and take a tour of all I have to show you. Until then, take pride in the house that is your home. Keep it neat and clean so that it is a pleasant place to live in. If you have a yard, plant flowers and trees in it. If you don't have a yard, grow a container garden in a window. If something in your house breaks, fix it right away. If something spills, clean it up right away too. After all, the place where you live is more than just some building – it's your home, and that makes it special.

Bibliography:

"White House." *Wikipedia*. October 12, 2012.
<en.wikipedia.org/wiki/The_White_House>

Clara Barton

History: Clara Barton was born on December 25, 1821 in North Oxford, Massachusetts. She is the founder of the American Red Cross and served as its president for 23 years. She died on April 12, 1912 at the age of 90 and is buried in Glen Echo, Maryland. Her dedication to helping others inspires us all to want

to volunteer and do what we can to share kindness with those in need.

Olivia was outside riding her bike when she saw a small dog limping along the sidewalk. She stopped her bike and the sweet natured dog approached her, wagging his tail. He nuzzled her hand and allowed her to pet him.

Olivia noticed that the little dog was holding up his right, front paw as if it were injured. She was very careful not to bump it or touch it, so she didn't hurt or upset him. After a while, she realized that it was getting late and she had better go home.

She got back on her bike and peddled home, but her new furry friend started to follow her.

"Go home!" she said to him, but the little dog just kept following her, limping behind as best as he could. The poor creature looked so tired and thirsty that her heart went out to it, and she let him follow her home.

When Olivia got to her house, she ran inside and told her parents about the inured animal. "Can I give him a bowl of water?"

Her parents said yes and went outside to inspect the dog. Olivia took one of her mother's best dishes and filled it with cool water for the hot animal. The dog lapped it up gratefully.

"Is that better?" Olivia smiled at the dog, as his tail wagged happily. Then she said to her parents, "his paw is definitely hurt. Maybe we should bring him inside to keep him safe."

"I think you're right," said her Dad. "We don't want him to get hit by a car limping in the street."

Olivia watched, fascinated, as her Dad checked the dogs injured paw. He saw that a sharp piece of glass was stuck there and carefully pulled it out. Olivia gave the dog pieces of cut up hotdog afterward to reward him for being so brave and good.

"Do you think we should put bandages on the paw, to help it heal?" Olivia asked her Dad.

"No, the paw will heal fine without it, but you're acting like a regular Clara Barton."

"Who's that?" Olivia asked.

Dad said, "Clara Barton helped soldiers in the Civil War and started the organization called the American Red Cross, but, when she was a little girl, she was a lot like you. She grew up on a farm in Oxford, Massachusetts. She loved animals and cared for them when they were injured. When her brother got hurt after falling from a barn, she helped care for him too.

"When she was a teenager, she worked as school teacher for fourteen years. She taught at a private school where wealthy parents could pay to send their children to be educated, but her heart went out to the poor children whose parents couldn't send their children to the school. So, what do you think she did?

"Clara Barton offered to teach those children without pay if the town would only provide her with a place to teach them. They agreed, and before long she had 600 students!

"When the Civil War began, she wanted to help the soldiers. She saw that many medical facilities didn't have enough bandages and supplies to care for the wounded men, so she collected donations and made bandages out of sheets and towels. The War Department gave her permission to go to the front lines of the battlefield to deliver her supplies and care for soldiers herself.

"People called her the 'Angel of the Battlefield' for her kindness. When the Civil War ended, she helped reunite thousands of soldiers with their families then went to Europe to help their wounded in the war between France and Prussia.

"In Europe, Clara discovered they had an organization called the International Red Cross. They helped deliver supplies and care to people in need. Clara dedicated herself to establishing a Red Cross in the United States. For eight years, she gave speeches and talked with people in government until she convinced them to allow her to form the American Red Cross.

"At first, the Red Cross only aided soldiers, but Clara soon discovered that people also needed help when they had been through disasters, such as floods and earthquakes, so she expanded the organization to help victims of disasters as well.

"Clara Barton served as the president of the American Red Cross for 23 years until she resigned at the age of 83. Since then, the organization has continued to grow and serve those in need. Each year, it strives to help people in need, from solitary victims of an apartment fire to those involved in massive tragedies like Hurricane Katrina. It is estimated that the American Red Cross serves 70,000 people a year and has a million volunteers and 30,000 employees."

"Wow!" Olivia said, her eyes big with wonder. "And you think I could be like Clara Barton?"

"I sure do." her Dad said. "Just look at the caring way you helped this dog. I predict that you're going to do a lot more volunteer work as you grow up."

Olivia smiled; she did like doing things to help others. She always helped their neighbor, Mrs. Cranshaw, rake her leaves in the fall and shovel the snow from her driveway in the winter. Mrs.

Cranshaw offered to pay her for it, but Olivia told her, "I don't want any money. I'm just one friend helping another."

Mrs. Cranshaw was really grateful, and it made Olivia feel really good inside.

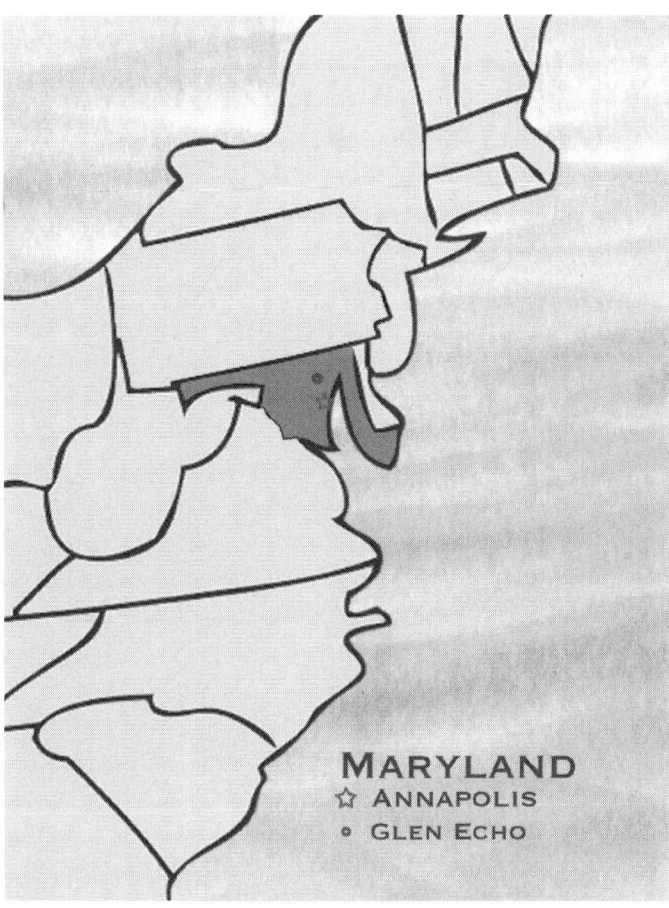

MARYLAND
☆ ANNAPOLIS
○ GLEN ECHO

When Olivia was collecting donations for her school's walkathon, Mrs. Cranshaw made an extra big donation as a way of saying thanks.

The next day, Olivia and her Dad were putting up posters saying they had found a lost dog when a family came running up to them. "That's Buster! We've been so worried about him!"

Olivia was a little sad to see the dog go, but she felt really good seeing how happy his family was to have him back and how happy he was to be back with them. His tail was wagging so fast that she thought he might fly away.

141

"Can we give you some reward money?" the mother of Buster's family asked.

Olivia looked at her Dad and said, "No money needed. Our reward is just knowing that we've helped."

Have you ever done anything to help someone like Olivia? Have you ever volunteered or raised donation money for a charity? It doesn't matter if what you are doing is big or small. As long as you're helping others, you'll feel good inside.

Bibliography:

"Clara Barton." *Garden of Praise*. October 12, 2012. <http://www.gardenofpraise.com>

"Clara Barton." *Wikipedia*. October 12, 2012. <http://en.wikipedia.org/wiki/Clara_Barton>

The Life of James Forten

History: James Forten lived from September 2, 1766 to March 4, 1842. He was an abolitionist, inventor, and philanthropist. He was a part of the American Colonization Society, which worked to free blacks from slavery. He purchased a newspaper called "The Liberator" and in 1813 wrote a pamphlet titled "Letters From a

Man of Colour." His incredible life story reminds us all of the power of kindness and friendship.

Billy was playing with his friends Miguel and Kai on the playground before school. They liked to climb up the metal bars of the jungle gym and race each other to the top.

"I win!" Billy called out, but Kai had already beaten him there.

Miguel was already at the top too. He said, "Actually, you came in third!"

The three friends laughed. It didn't matter which of them came in first, second, or third. The truth was that they just liked playing together.

A new boy in class came up to them. He said, "Hi, I'm Seth. Can I play too?"

"Sorry, there's only room here for three." Billy said. Seth looked sad and walked off.

Miguel frowned at Billy and said, "Why did you tell him that? There's plenty of room for one more friend."

"Yeah," Kai agreed. "No one deserves to be left out."

Billy thought about what his two friends were saying. Maybe they were right. He thought about the lesson they had just learned in class about James Forten.

James Forten was born in Philadelphia, Pennsylvania on September 2, 1766. His grandfather had been a slave, but he managed to obtain his freedom. James' parents, Thomas and Sarah Forten, were free black Americans, and so was James.

When he was eight years old, he starting working with his father at Robert Bridges sail loft. Can you imagine going to work every day at that age? A year later, James' father fell into the Delaware River during an accident and drowned.

When James was 14, he went to work on a sailing ship called the Royal Lewis as a powder boy. During that time, he was captured by an English ship and played the game of marbles with the captain's son. They became good friends, and the captain's son would not let his father sell James as a slave. James used to say that a game of marbles saved his life, but really it was friendship!

Eventually, James was released and allowed to return home, where he once again went to work for Mr. Bridges making sails. He was a smart young man and a hard worker, so over time he was promoted to the position of foreman.

In 1798, Mr. Bridges retired, and he loaned James enough money to be able to buy his business and become the owner. Now James Forten was the boss of 38 employees. He invented a different type of sail that was

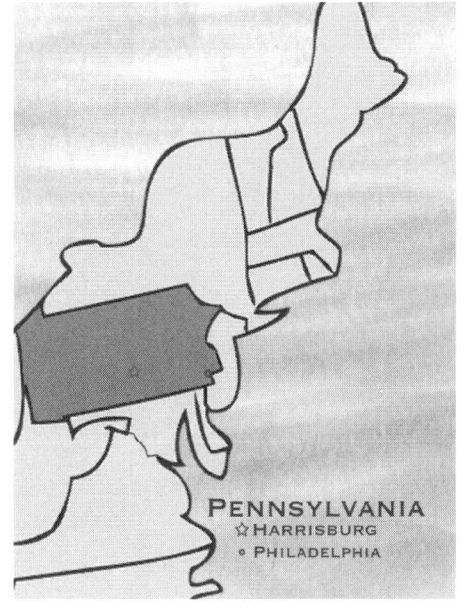

capable of maneuvering more easily and became a huge financial success. The grandson of a former slave, James Forten was now a very wealthy business man.

James remembered how friendships had helped save his life, and he wanted to do the same for others. He used his fortune to buy freedom for slaves, opened a school for black children, and allowed the Underground Railroad to use his home as a depot to bring escaping slaves to freedom.

Thinking about James Forten's incredible life and also thinking about what his friends, Miguel and Kai, had said made Billy realize the importance of friendship. What if the boy on the boat hadn't invited James to play marbles with him? What if James hadn't been willing to open his home to others?

Billy looked at his friends and said, "You're right. There's always room for one more friend. Let's go find Seth and invite him to come play with us!"

The three boys jumped down to the ground from the jungle gym and went searching for Seth. They found him all alone, sitting under a tree. He looked very sad and lonely, and they felt bad that they had turned him away.

Billy said, "I didn't mean what I said before. There's always room for another friend. Will you come and play with us?"

Seth got up slowly and looked at them with surprise.

"Yeah, come and play with us!" Kai and Miguel said together.

Seth grinned and said, "Race you to the top!" The four boys ran together, laughing and having fun.

When someone asks you to play with them, what do you say?

Bibliography:

"James Forten." *The Black Inventor Online Museum*. October 11, 2012.
<www.blackinventor.com/pages/james-forten.html>

"James Forten." *Garden of Praise, Inventors*. October 11, 2012.
<http://www.gardenofpraise.com/>

The Letter

History: Thomas Jefferson was a Founding Father of the United States. He was the principal author of the Declaration of Independence, served in the Continental Congress, was Secretary of State from 1790 to 1793, was Vice President from 1797 to 1801,

and was the third President of the U.S. As President, he served for two terms and was in office from March 4, 1801 to March 4, 1809. During his presidency, he oversaw the Louisiana Purchase, greatly expanding the size of the country. Listen to his story and learn why the art of letter writing is something none of us should forget.

Every year, Sarah and Johnny's Aunt Roberta sent them a present in the mail on their birthday. She also sent them presents for Christmas. They loved opening the packages and unwrapping the toys inside. Aunt Roberta always gave the best presents! There was just one thing they didn't like.

Every time Sarah and Johnny got a gift from Aunt Roberta, they could always count on hearing their mother say, "Don't forget to write her a thank you note."

"Do we have to, Mom?" Sarah complained. She didn't want to have to stop playing with her new doll just to write a stupid letter.

Johnny thought he'd found a clever way to solve problem. He waved a folded piece of paper in the air and said, "I've already written mine."

"Terrific! Just let me read it really quick." Mom grabbed the piece of paper and unfolded it. She read the entire letter in just two seconds. All he had written was "Thanks! Love, Johnny."

Mom gave Johnny a very disappointed frown. She put her hands on her hips and looked at both her children with a serious expression.

"I want you both to write Aunt Roberta a true letter, telling her honestly how much you love the gifts she gave you and thanking her for them. You may think it's a waste of time, but she will really appreciate it. Letters mean more to people than you may realize.

"Just think of Thomas Jefferson. He understood the importance of writing. If he hadn't, none of us would be where we are today."

"What does he have to do with writing letters?" Sarah asked with a confused look. "Wasn't he the third president of the United States?"

"Yes," Johnny said, not wanting his sister to appear smarter than he was. "He started out as a lawyer in Virginia. After we won our independence, he was the Secretary of State for President George Washington. After that, he became Vice President under John Adams and was then elected the third President of the U.S. in 1801."

Sarah didn't like her brother showing off, so she said, "Well all that is really important, but what does it have to do with writing thank you notes?"

Johnny opened his mouth to answer, but he really couldn't think of anything to say. He clamped his mouth back shut, and they both looked at their mother. Speaking at the exact same time, Sarah and Johnny both asked her, "So what does Thomas Jefferson have to do with writing thank you notes?"

What do you think the answer is?

Mom smiled at the both of them and said, "Thomas Jefferson did all those things, but, long before he could, our nation had to fight for its independence first. When Jefferson was growing up, the thirteen colonies were still under British rule, and a lot of people were unhappy about it, including him.

"He had become a very good writer, so he wrote letters trying to help the colonies become an independent nation. He wrote letter after letter, with some experts estimating that he wrote 50,000 letters during the course of his lifetime.

"When the colonists decided that they were ready to fight for their freedom, they chose five men to write the Declaration of Independence. Thomas Jefferson was one of the men chosen for the task. Can you imagine how he must have felt?

"He knew that this was a writing job of great importance, and

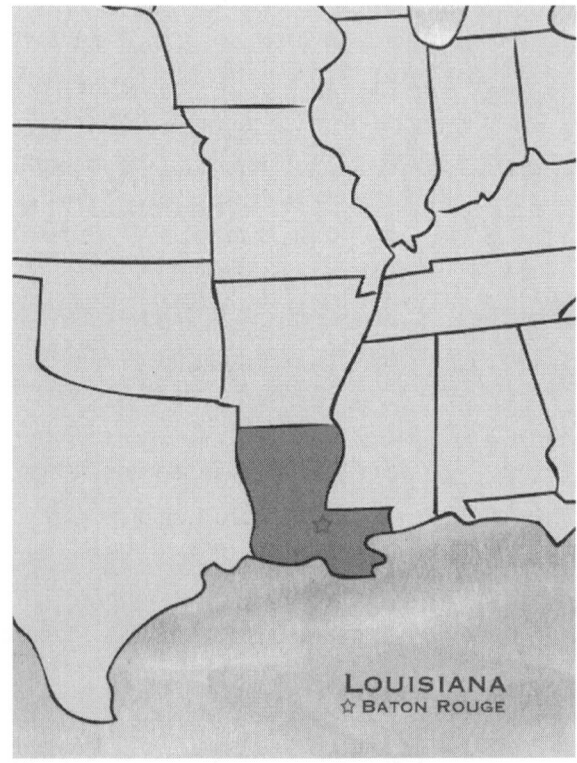

he wanted to do his very best. He needed quiet to be able to concentrate, so he rented a house and stayed in it for seventeen days, completely by himself."

Sarah looked at the ground, feeling guilty. She had been complaining about writing one little letter, and Jefferson had been willing to work so hard. Johnny felt embarrassed about the pitiful note he'd written to his aunt.

LOUISIANA
☆ BATON ROUGE

Mom said, "The words Jefferson wrote helped inspire the colonists to fight for their freedom. His words shaped our nation and made America what it is today. Writing letters has the power to touch people's lives in amazing ways. So, when you have the opportunity to write someone a letter, do it with your heart and your mind and give it your best effort."

Sarah and Johnny each wrote their Aunt Roberta a real thank you letter that told her how much they appreciated the gifts she had sent them and how much they loved her and were glad she was their aunt. When she received the letters, she was deeply touched by their thoughtful words and kept them in a special drawer.

Many years later, Sarah and Johnny grew up to have children of their own. They always sent each other's children gifts for their birthdays and Christmas, and they always had their children write a real letter to say thank you.

"Do I have to write Aunt Sarah a thank you letter?" Johnny's daughter little, Roberta, asked him.

He just smiled at her and prepared to tell her the story of Thomas Jefferson, one of the greatest letter writers in history.

Bibliography:

"Thomas Jefferson." *Famous Leaders for Young Readers, Garden of Praise*. October 12, 2012. <http://www.gardenofpraise.com/>

"Thomas Jefferson." *Wikipedia*. October 12, 2012. <http://en.wikipedia.org/wiki/Thomas_jefferson>

The Power of Money

History: The Constitution of the United States of America allows that the U.S. Congress has the power to create money for the purpose of conducting trade and commerce. Under the Coinage Act of 1792, Congress built the U.S. Mint as part of the Department of

Treasury. During the Civil War, Congress authorized the Secretary of the Treasury to start issuing paper currency in lieu of coins. The Bureau of Engraving and Printing (BEP) is responsible for printing all paper currency, while the U.S. mint makes all coins.

"The glow of one warm thought is to me worth more than money." That's a famous quote by me, Thomas Jefferson. I said it so people would understand that good thoughts and how people treat each other are more important than money.

It's funny, but today my picture is actually printed on money. You'll find me on the $2 bill and also on the nickel coin (5¢). As much as I want people to remember that money isn't the most important thing in the world, it is a great honor and shows respect for my efforts in writing the Declaration of Independence and serving as the third President of the U.S.

The first president of the U.S., of course, got the honor of being on the $1 bill. Do you know who that is? Of course – President George Washington. His face is also on the quarter coin (25¢). His portrait for the $1 bill was painted by Gilbert Stuart. The average "life" of a $1 bill is twenty two months, just short of two years. By then, the $1 bill has been passed around to so many people and used so much that it has gotten too worn out and needs to be destroyed. That's why new bills are constantly being printed by the Bureau of Engraving and Printing (BEP). Americans use $1 bills so much and are printing new ones so often that 45% of all money produced is $1 bills. Isn't that amazing?

I bet you know whose picture appears on the $5 bill. I'll give you a clue – it's the same man who also appears on the penny (1¢). That's right – President Abraham Lincoln, who was our nation's sixteenth president and the one who ended slavery in the country and saw us through the Civil War.

It's interesting that the $10 bill is one of the few amounts of currency that does not have a picture of a U.S. president on it. The $10 bill had a picture of Alexander Hamilton. I bet you're wondering why someone who wasn't a president could have his picture on money. Alexander Hamilton was a founding father and our nation's very first Secretary of the Treasury. Since that is the position in charge of our nation's currency, I'm sure it is only right that they would want to honor the first man to hold that post.

President Andrew Jackson appears on the $20 bill, and President Ulysses S. Grant appears on the $50 bill. Both were great men whose service to this country deserves to be honored.

For the $100 bill, another great man appears, but it is the second currency that does not depict a U.S. president. The $100 bill has a picture of Benjamin Franklin. His face also appears on the fifty cent coin, also referred to as the half dollar. Franklin may not have been a president, but he played a very important role in our history as a founding father and gained fame for his many experiments with electricity. He was a brilliant inventor and scientist, as well as a politician and diplomat. Do you think he was a good choice for the $100 bill?

These bills that I mentioned are the most common and used by most people. You've probably seen most of them, although the $2 bill is less common. Many people consider them to bring good luck and like to hang onto them, although that's just superstition of course.

The U.S. Treasury also created currency of larger denominations to make it easier for banks, businesses, and people who were wealthy. There is a $500 dollar bill showing President William McKinley, a $1000 bill showing President Grover Cleveland, and a $5000 bill showing President James Madison. Can you imagine what it must be like to have stack of those? I think I would want to do something with it to help others. How about you?

154

There is a $10,000 bill showing a man named Salmon P. Chase. This is the third and final bill to depict a man who was not a U.S. President. Chase was the Secretary of the Treasury for President Lincoln. Later, he became the sixth Chief Justice of the U.S. Supreme Court.

President Woodrow Wilson has the honor of appearing on our nation's largest denomination of currency, which is the $100,000 dollar bill. There is no such thing as a million dollar bill, although there have been lots of them made for fun. Sometimes criminals will try to use a million dollar bill to trick people, but they don't get very far before they're

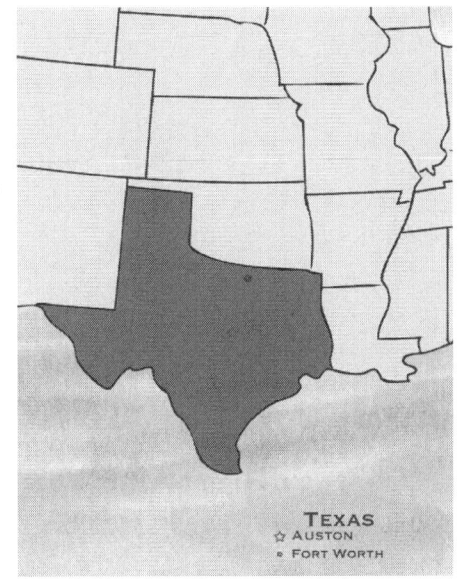

arrested. Many people enjoy buying fake million dollar bills from stores to be silly. Have you ever seen one in a store?

If they did make a million dollar bill for real, whose picture do you think should go on it? I don't think I would want my picture there because, as I've already said, there are much more important things than money. Can you name some of them?

Bibliography:

"Presidents on Money." *Marshu*. October 18, 2012. <marshu.com/articles/presidents-on-us-united-states-paper-bills-currency.php>

"Quotes about Money." *Brainy Quote*. October 18, 2012. <www.brainyquote.com/quotes/keywords/money.html#J9mq4cYlFhKhrIiJ.99>

Mark Twain

History: Mark Twain was the pen name of Samuel Langhorne Clemens, a well known American author and humorist. He was born on November 30, 1835 in Florida, Missouri. His novel, The Adventures of Tom Sawyer, *was considered by many to be "the*

great American novel." He died on April 21, 1910 at the age of 74 in Redding, Connecticut.

Julie was doing a report on a famous author for school. She picked Mark Twain because he had written *The Prince and The Pauper*, which was one of her favorite stories. It was the tale of a wealthy prince and a poor boy, called a pauper, who looked so much like each other that they were able to switch places with one another, and great adventure followed. Mark Twain wrote many other books, including *The Adventures of Tom Sawyer* and *The Adventures of Huckleberry Finn.* You may have seen movies about them or read adaptations of the stories made for children. They're full of adventure and excitement.

Julie learned that Mark Twain's real name was Samuel Clemens and that he had been born on November 30, 1835 in the town of Florida, Missouri. As Julie worked on her report, she thought about how many books Mark Twain had written, 28 in total plus many short stories and essays. She thought to herself, "I bet he always knew he wanted to be a writer. I wish I knew what I want to be when I grew up. I can never decide."

Julie's idea was confirmed when she learned that Clemens was just thirteen years old when he became a printer's apprentice. Just two years later, he got a job as a printer and editorial assistant for his brother Orion's newspaper. That was when he got his first taste for writing and found that he enjoyed it. Julie felt bad because she didn't know what she had a taste for yet. Shouldn't she know what she is good at and liked doing by now? Have you ever felt like that?

What Julie learned next really surprised her! She thought for sure that Clemens would begin his writing career while working at the newspaper, but he did just the opposite. At the age of 17, he became a river pilot's apprentice and learned how to operate steamboats. Julie was shocked! How could a boy who would grow up to be a famous author leave printing to become a steamboat pilot?

It turned out that Clemens was on his way to St. Louis for a printer's job, when he found he had a real ability for piloting steamboats. That is where his famous nick name came from. The words "mark twain" are a river boating term; they mean that the river has a depth of two fathoms, so the water is deep enough for a boat to safely navigate. Clemens got his river pilot's license in 1858 and worked on steamboats for years.

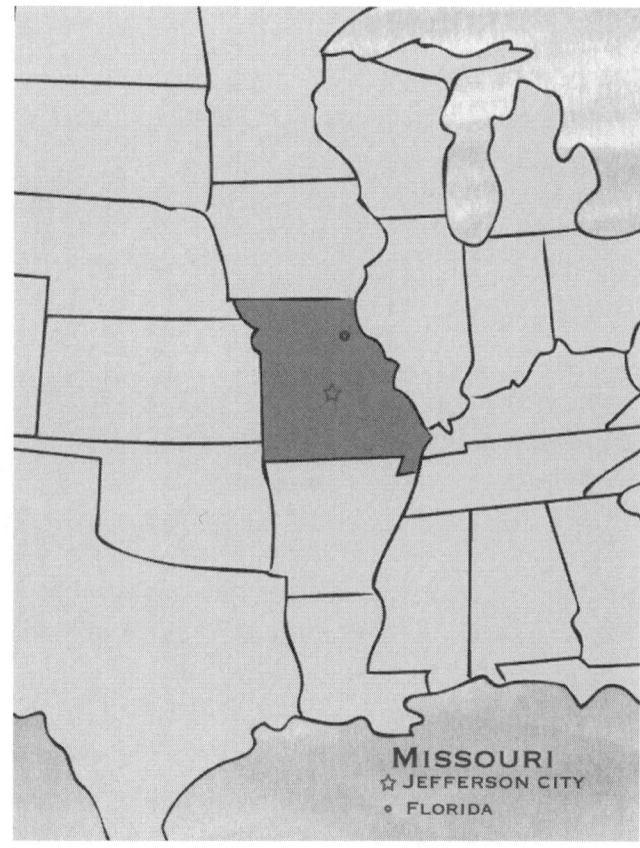

Traders made steamboats a very big business until the Civil War in 1861, and then it came to a standstill and he could no longer make a living that way. So, Clemens started working as a reporter for several newspapers across the United States. Julie wondered if the steamboat business had stayed strong, would Clemens have done that forever and never have gone back to writing. What do you think?

As a writer, Clemens wanted a pen-name or pseudonym, so he started writing under the name Mark Twain. His first book, *The Innocents Abroad*, was published in 1869. It didn't take long for his writing career to really take off, making Mark Twain one of the most famous writers in American culture.

As Julie finished her report, she continued to be amazed that Mark Twain had been a printer's apprentice, a steamboat pilot, and finally a writer. He hadn't published his first book until he was 34 years old. Maybe it wasn't such a big deal that she didn't know what she wanted to be when grew up yet. Maybe she had plenty of time to learn new things and see what all the different careers were that the world had to offer. Maybe there was something great out there that she hadn't heard of yet or would discover as she grew up.

Bibliography:

Official Website of Mark Twain. October 17, 2012.
<http://cmgww.com/historic/twain/>

"Mark Twain." *Wikipedia*. October 17, 2012.
<http://en.wikipedia.org/wiki/Mark_Twain>

Jason and the Cherry Tree

History: The legendary story of George Washington and the Cherry Tree, which credits Washington with saying, "I cannot tell a lie," was written by Mason Locke Weems. He was an American author, known as Parson Weems. The famous story is included in

his book The Life of Washington *(1800). His work was not verifiable and has come to be considered an American fable or folklore. They continue to bring joy to children even now, imparting patriotism and values just as they did when they were first written. Read the story along with a child in your life and see if they learn the same lesson on truth and obeying one's parents as Jason does.*

"Jason, don't play ball in the house!" Mom said, as her son left his room wearing his favorite baseball glove and holding a ball.

"Okay, Mom," Jason said, but, as soon as he was out of her sight, he gave the ball a little toss in the air and caught it easily in his glove. Mom worried too much. Catching a baseball was easy. He could do it without even looking.

To prove the point to himself, he closed his eyes and gave the ball a small toss in the air. Do you think this was a good idea?

Jason heard the sound of the ball hitting the floor. He opened his eyes and looked down at the ground. The ball was nowhere to be seen. Jason realized it must have rolled away.

He looked under the table, but it wasn't there. He got down on his hands and knees and looked under the chairs, but it wasn't there. He crawled through the doorway to the next room and crawled into a pair of familiar shoes. Jason looked up to see his father staring down at him. Dad was holding his baseball in his hands.

"Son, we're you playing ball in the house?"

Jason didn't know what to say. He didn't want to get into trouble, but he knew that he really had been playing in the house. He started to shake his head no, and, as he did, he saw a book sitting on the table. It gave him a good idea.

Jason said, "Dad, can you please read me a story?"

Dad knew that Jason was avoiding answering the question, but he had an idea too.

Dad said, "Sure. Let me read you my favorite story. It's called *The Cherry Tree,* and it was written a long time ago by a man named Parson M.L. Weems. It's about President George Washington when he was just a boy your age."

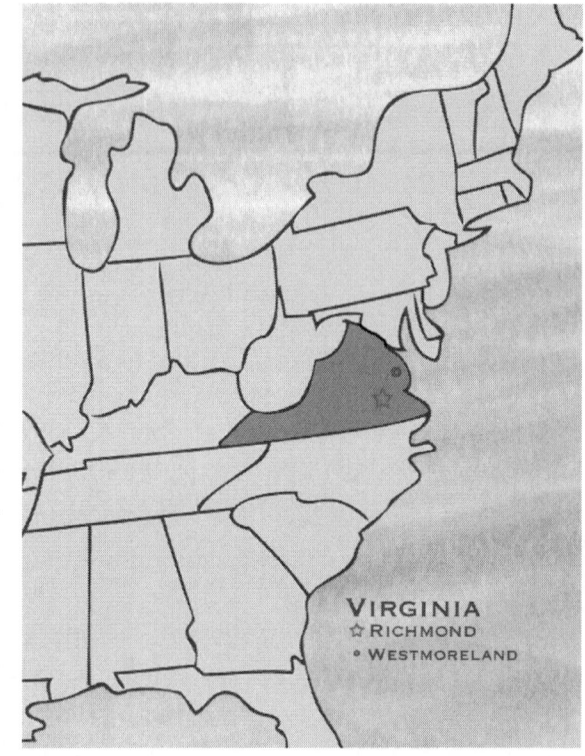

VIRGINIA
☆ RICHMOND
• WESTMORELAND

Dad sat on the couch and Jason sat by his side. Dad opened the book to the story and read it. It went just like this:

"The Cherry Tree, by M.L. Weems

"When George was about six years old, he was made the wealthy master of a hatchet of which, like most little boys, he was extremely fond. He went about chopping everything that came his way.

"One day, as he wandered about the garden amusing himself by hacking his mother's pea sticks, he found a beautiful, young English cherry tree, of which his father was most proud. He tried the edge of his hatchet on the trunk of the tree and barked it so that it died.

"Some time after this, his father discovered what had happened to his favorite tree. He came into the house in great anger and demanded to know who the mischievous person was who had cut away the bark. Nobody could tell him anything about it.

"Just then George, with his little hatchet, came into the room.

"'George,' said his father, 'do you know who has killed my beautiful little cherry tree yonder in the garden? I would not have taken five guineas for it!'"

"This was a hard question to answer, and for a moment George was staggered by it, but quickly recovering himself he cried:

"'I cannot tell a lie, father, you know I cannot tell a lie! I did cut it with my little hatchet.'"

"The anger died out of his father's face, and taking the boy tenderly in his arms, he said:

"'My son, that you should not be afraid to tell the truth is more to me than a thousand trees! Yes - though they were blossomed with silver and had leaves of the purest gold!'"

When Dad was finished, he closed the book and looked at Jason. Dad said, "So tell me, son, what do you think of that story?"

"It was good." Jason said. He couldn't believe that boys his age used to be allowed to play with hatchets. He much preferred playing catch with his baseball. Then another thought occurred to him.

Jason looked at his Dad and said, "I cannot tell a lie, either. Dad, I was playing ball in the house, even though I knew I shouldn't."

Dad looked very serious, and Jason worried that he would be in trouble. Dad said, "I'm very proud of you for telling me the truth. Being honest is very important. Obeying the rules is very important too, and I'm not pleased that you disobeyed the rule about not playing ball in the house. Suppose you had broken something."

Jason looked at his feet. He knew his Dad was right. Dad said, "Give me a hug and promise me that from now on you will not only be honest, but obey the rules too."

"I promise!" Jason said, and he meant it with all his heart. The next day, Mom saw Jason leaving his bedroom with his glove and his ball.

"Don't play ball in the house!" she said.

"Okay, Mom." Jason said. He rounded the corner and was out of her sight. He picked up the ball and prepared to toss it into the air, but suddenly he remembered his promise to Dad and the story of George Washington and the Cherry Tree.

"I'm going outside!" Jason called to his Mom. He opened the door and went out in the yard. It felt good to be out in the fresh air, playing with his ball. It felt even better knowing that he had upheld his promise.

Bibliography:

"The Cherry Tree." *Printable Presidents Day Stories, Tales and Legends, George Washington.* October 17, 2012. <www.apples4theteacher.com/holidays/presidents-day/george-washington/short-stories/the-cherry-tree.html>

"M. L. Weems." *Wikipedia.* October 17, 2012. <en.wikipedia.org/wiki/M._L._Weems>

Nathan Hale

History: Nathan Hale was born on June 6, 1755 in Coventry, Connecticut. He was a soldier for the Continental Army during the American Revolutionary War, when he was captured as a spy. His last words became legendary, elevating him to hero status. He died

on September 22, 1776 in New York City when he was hung by the British. Statues and memorials of him can be found throughout the U.S. Let his inspiring tale remind us all of why freedom is worth dying for.

Tommy and Luis were playing soldier. Tommy crawled through the grass, hiding under a bush. He couldn't see Luis anywhere, but he knew he must be close. His ears listened for any sound, but all he heard was the rustle of leaves in the trees.

"I found you!" Luis shouted excitedly, as he jumped out from behind a bush and pointed at Tommy. Clearly captured, Tommy got up and stood with his hands in the air, as if surrendering to the enemy.

Tommy said, "I regret that I have but one life to give for my country." The two boys laughed.

Luis tagged Tommy on the shoulder and said, "now you're it!" The two friends chased each other around the yard, laughing and having fun the rest of the afternoon.

That night, when Luis' mom was tucking him in bed, he asked her, "Mom, what does 'I regret that I have but one life to give for my country' mean?"

"What?" His mother looked confused.

Luis explained about the game of soldier and tag that he and Tommy had been playing, ending with the part when Tommy quoted the famous phrase. "So, what does it mean?" Luis wanted to know.

"Well, it's a famous phrase that was first said by Nathan Hale, who was a soldier in the Revolutionary War," Mom explained. "He had been born on June 6, 1755 in Coventry, Connecticut. When he was just thirteen years old, he went to Yale College and graduated in 1773. He worked as a teacher until the Revolutionary War began in 1775, and he joined a Connecticut militia.

"One day in September 1776, General George Washington said that he needed a spy to go into enemy territory and tell him where they were located. Nathan Hale was the only soldier to volunteer for this dangerous mission.

"Although he must have been very scared, on September 12 Hale took a ferry across the river to Manhattan Island to spy on the British. The war was not going well for the colonial army, and the British were taking over New York. Much of it was burned in the Great New York Fire of 1776, although no one knows if this was caused by the British or the Americans.

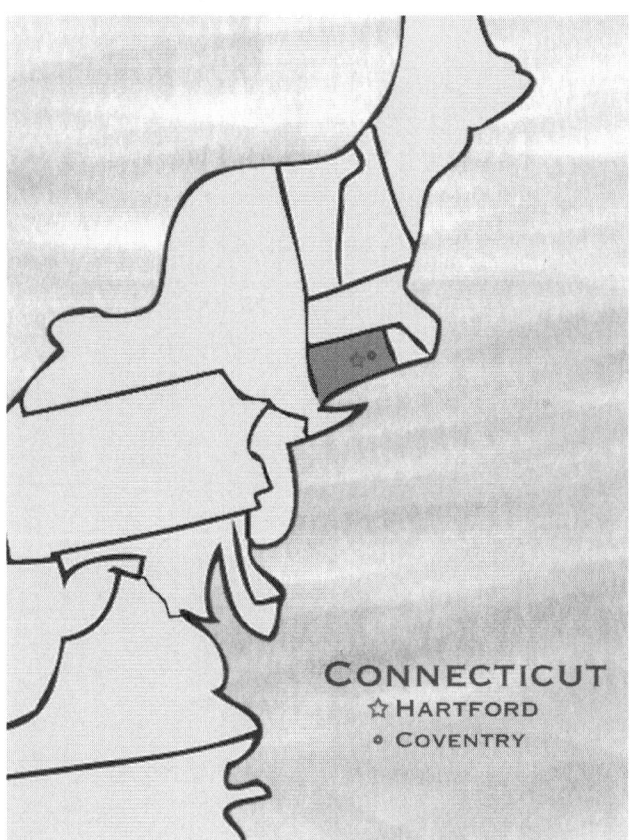

CONNECTICUT
☆ HARTFORD
○ COVENTRY

"Nathan Hale became captured by the British. They knew he was a spy, which was a crime that was punishable by death. On the morning of September 22, 1776, Nathan Hale was to be hanged. He was only 21 years old. Just before he was hung, Nathan Hale made the famous speech, saying 'I only regret that I have but one life to give for my country.' Do you know what that means?"

Luis wasn't sure. He thought about it for a long time. What do you think it might mean?

Luis' mother said, "It means that he believed in the freedom that the Confederates were fighting for in the Revolutionary War. He believed in it so much that he didn't mind dying for it. In fact, he believed in it so much that he would die again if he could and that it was too bad he only had one life because, if he had more lives, he would be willing to die for his country every time."

"Wow!" Luis said. "Why did he believe in freedom so much?"

"Well, freedom is a pretty terrific thing," Mom said. "If you don't have it, you really wish you did. Think about all the things that you're free to do because you are an American citizen."

Luis thought and started to write out a list. He wrote down "Freedom to go to school, freedom to live where I want to, freedom to work the kind of job I want when I grow up, and the freedom to marry who I want." What other freedoms can you think of that Americans have?

Bibliography:

"Nathan Hale." *The Connecticut Society of the Sons of the American Revolution.* October 19, 2012. <http://www.connecticutsar.org/patriots/hale_nathan.htm>

"Nathan Hale." *Wikipedia.* October 19, 2012. <http://en.wikipedia.org/wiki/Nathan_Hale>

Great Ideals

History: The mountain originally called "Six Grandfathers" by the Lakota Sioux was renamed by lawyer Charles E. Rushmore in 1885 during an expedition. The project of carving the mountain into a monument received congressional approval under the

presidency of Calvin Coolidge. Carving began in 1927 and was completed in 1941. Surprisingly, no workers were killed during the entire project. Mount Rushmore is one of the greatest sculptures ever made, and it will inspire you to find the creative side within yourself.

Check it out! This is the famous Mount Rushmore. Isn't it amazing? It's located near Keystone, South Dakota. It is a giant sculpture of four U.S. presidents: George Washington, Thomas Jefferson, Theodore Roosevelt, and Abraham Lincoln. They are each 60 feet tall and comprised mostly of granite. If the bodies could be built to scale, they would be men who were 465 feet tall!

I bet you're wondering why those four presidents were chosen. They each represent a specific ideal of what makes America so great. George Washington represents independence, as he was the one who lead us to victory in the War of Independence against the British, and of course he was also our first president. I wonder if George Washington thinks it's cooler to be on Mount Rushmore or to have his face on the quarter and the dollar. Which do you think would be more exciting?

Thomas Jefferson represents democracy, as he was one of the founding fathers who created our form of government. He was the principle author of the Declaration of Independence and later became our nation's third President. I bet he never imagined that one day there would be a 60 foot sculpture of his head on the side on a mountain! I wonder what he would say if he could see it!

Theodore Roosevelt represents our nation's leadership in world affairs. As the twenty sixth president of the United States, he led our country in the progressive movement, conservation of nature, and also in assisting other countries. He won the Nobel Peace Prize for his efforts. His family and friends called him Teddy. He was an avid hunter, and one day he saw a bear that was hurt in the woods. He did not want the bear to suffer and had it killed. After that famous story, a toy company that made stuffed bears asked if they could name their toy the Teddy Bear. The name took, and today most people refer to all stuffed bears as Teddy Bears after the famous President. Do you have a teddy bear? I bet you never knew where the name came from! Now you can tell your bear!

Abraham Lincoln represents equality. He was the sixteenth president of the United States during a time when people were forced to be slaves. President Lincoln knew that all people should be treated equal and put an end to slavery. The South refused, and Civil War broke out. Lincoln refused to let injustice continue, won the war, and freed all the slaves. Who knows what other great things he could have accomplished had he not been assassinated? Lincoln's face also appears on the penny, and there is a huge statue of him at the Lincoln Memorial in Washington D.C. That statue is 19 feet tall, which is pretty big, but not near as big as his sculpture on Mount Rushmore.

Together, these four great men representing the ideals of independence, democracy, world affairs, and equality also represent the first 150 years of our country's history. A historian named Doan Robinson came up with the idea for the great monument in 1923 to promote tourism in South Dakota. He hired sculptor Gutzon Borglum to create it. He has created many other statues for National Monuments and Universities. Do you like looking at statues?

On October 4, 1927 the work began. Four hundred workers assisted throughout the length of the project, and none of them were killed during the dangerous job, which is amazing for that time. Can you guess how long it took them to complete it? It was finished in just 14 years, on October 31, 1941. That's pretty incredible when you think about how huge it is! Have you ever made anything out of clay or dough? Have you ever carved anything out of wood or rock? It's no easy task!

Today, Mount Rushmore is a very popular tourist attraction, and millions have been to see it. I wonder what those four great Presidents must think of that. I bet it makes them feel proud that so many people continue to feel pride in their country and want to uphold the ideals that they represent.

What does the ideal of independence mean to you? How about democracy, world affairs, and equality? Think about what kind of monument you would have built to represent those four things. Would you have made a sculpture or a painting? Would you have written a song or drawn a picture? Think of ways that you can express the

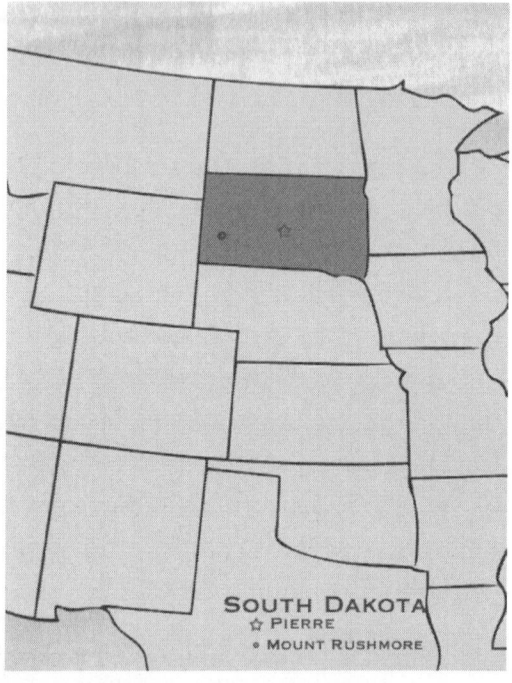

great ideals of America and make something that represents it.

It doesn't need to be big. In fact, I'm sure your parents don't want you making a giant sculpture in your back yard! However, something small can be just as meaningful. Just get an ordinary piece of paper or a regular lump of clay and make something great that means America to you.

Bibliography:

Mount Rushmore. October 19, 2012. <http://www.mtrushmore.net/index.html>

"Mount Rushmore." *New World Encyclopedia.* October 19, 2012.
<http://www.newworldencyclopedia.org/entry/Mount_Rushmore>

The Hull House and Me

History: Jane Addams was born on September 6, 1860 in Cedarville, Illinois. She dedicated her life to social and political activism and philanthropy. She co-founded the Hull House in 1889. Later, she became the first American woman to be awarded with a Nobel Peace Prize. She died on May 21, 1935 at the age of 74 in

Chicago, Illinois. Her story will inspire you to want to do more within your community.

Hi, my name is Jane Addams. I was born on September 6, in 1860. I don't remember my mother because she died when I was just two years old. I loved my father, though, very much. We lived in a fancy house in the country, and my father worked as a businessman. He owned lots of mills that processed timber, flour, and even wool. There was nothing I loved more than going with him in our carriage as he visited his mills. After he was finished taking care of work, he would often take me to the candy store for a treat. Have you ever gone with your parents to their work?

One day, my father was visiting one of his mills that was located in a very poor part of the city. I couldn't believe what I saw. Children, the same age as me, wearing nothing but dirty rags, playing in the street. They had no toys, and they looked hungry and thin. Their houses were very small and run-down. They looked like they would be cold in the winter. I asked my Daddy about them, and he explained that they had to live that way because they were poor. I realized then and there how lucky I was.

Before that moment, I didn't always think of myself as lucky. When I was very young, I became sick with tuberculosis, and the illness caused my spine to curve. I thought that it made me look hideous and that my father would be embarrassed to call me his daughter. Of course, he never was. He loved me just as I was. Seeing the poor and hungry children living in broken houses made me realize that there were people in the world with problems much bigger than just having a crooked back. I vowed then and there that one day I would help them.

When I grew up, my father sent me to college. I graduated in 1881 and wanted to do something useful with all the knowledge I had learned, but I wasn't sure what. When my father died, I inherited a large fortune and traveled to Europe. While I was in London, England, I learned that they had special places that offered programs to help the poor. I knew that's what I wanted to do with my life!

In 1889, my friend Ellen Gates Starr and I rented an old run-down mansion in one of the poorest neighborhoods in Chicago. It

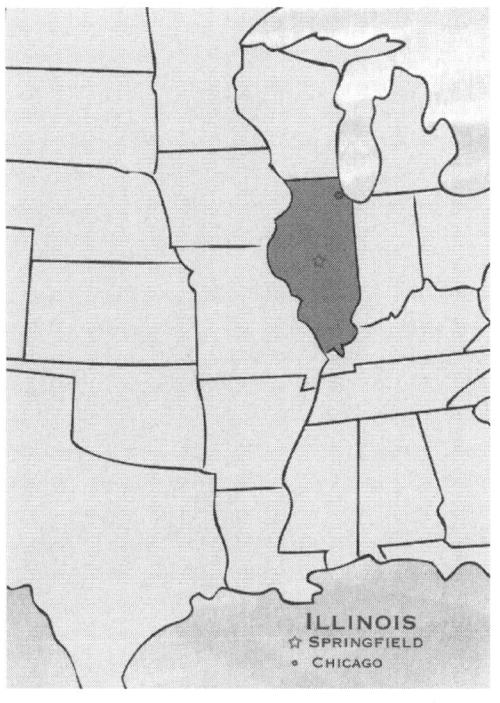

had belonged to a man named Charles Hull, so everyone called it Hull House. The people that lived in the neighborhood around Hull House were mostly immigrants. They lived in terrible housing called tenements and worked in nearby factories that paid them very little wages. The mothers could not afford to hire anyone to care for their children when they had to go to work, so the little ones would be left alone in the tenements, and the older ones would often have to go work themselves in sweatshops. The conditions were so terrible that it broke my heart! Can you imagine having to work in a sweatshop to feed your family?

I wanted Hull House to make their lives better. The first thing I did was to create a day-care center there, where people could bring their young children. They would be safely cared for and receive at least one meal at day. For older children, I established a kindergarten and a boys club. Eventually, I opened a coffee shop where adults could relax and enjoy a cup of brew. Other women in my social circle saw what I was doing and volunteered to help. It felt good to be serving our community in such a positive way and making people's lives better. Have you ever gone to a boys or girls club? They're a lot of fun and full of kids and great activities.

Over time, I realized I needed to do more than just run Hull House if I was going to make a difference in people's lives. I started a campaign to improve the working conditions in sweatshops. When the manufacturers association offered to donate $50,000 to Hull House if I dropped my campaign, I refused the bribe and became more determined than ever. Do you think you would have taken the bribe?

My hard work paid off, and in 1893 Illinois passed a workshop bill banning the exploitation of children in factories. I didn't quit there and dedicated my life to helping children, women, and the poor, including the development of juvenile courts and women's suffrage. What causes are important to you?

In 1931, I was awarded the Nobel Peace Prize. It was a huge honor, and I was the first woman to be given the prize, which is another honor in itself. What do you think you could do to help people in your community?

Bibliography:

"Hull House." *Encyclopedia of Chicago*. October 18, 2012. <http://www.encyclopedia.chicagohistory.org/pages/615.html>

"Hull House." *Wikipedia*. October 18, 2012. <http://en.wikipedia.org>

The Songs of Mahalia Jackson

History: Mahalia Jackson was born on October 26, 1911 to John A. Jackson and Charity Clark. Her powerful voice earned her the nickname "The Queen of Gospel" and garnered her 30 albums, including a dozen gold records. She was an important part of the

Civil Rights Movement, using her songs to inspire and raise funds. She died on January 27, 1972 of heart failure in her home in Evergreen Park, Illinois. Her story will make you want to sing the songs that are in your heart and not just the songs you think others want to hear.

"Are you going to audition for the school play?" Miguel asked his sister, Anna.

"I don't know," Anna said, shuffling her feet.

"You should." Miguel said. "You're a really good singer and actress. I know you'd get a part."

"Thanks, but I don't know what to sing at the audition. I think I'll just skip it."

"Just sing one of the songs you're always singing at home or at church." Miguel said.

"Those are all gospel songs." Anna shook her head. "What if people laugh at me for singing them at the audition?"

"I don't think anybody will laugh." Miguel said. "Gospel songs are great pieces of music and, if they're what you like to sing, then that's what you should sing."

"Do you really think so?" Anna asked.

"Of course!" Miguel said. "When you sing the kind of songs that you love, it comes through in your voice. Why, you could even be the next Mahalia Jackson."

"Really?" Anna asked, her eyes shining bright. Mahalia Jackson was one of her favorite singers, even though she lived long ago. She'd been born way back on October 26, 1911 in New Orleans, Louisiana. Her father, John A. Jackson, had been a barber and a preacher. Her mother, Charity Clark, died when Mahalia was only four years old, so her father sent her to live with her aunt Mahalia "Duke" Paul. Even though she was very young, Mahalia loved to sing hymns and gospel tunes to her Aunt Duke and at the Plymouth Rock Baptist Church, where they attended services. Do you like to sing too?

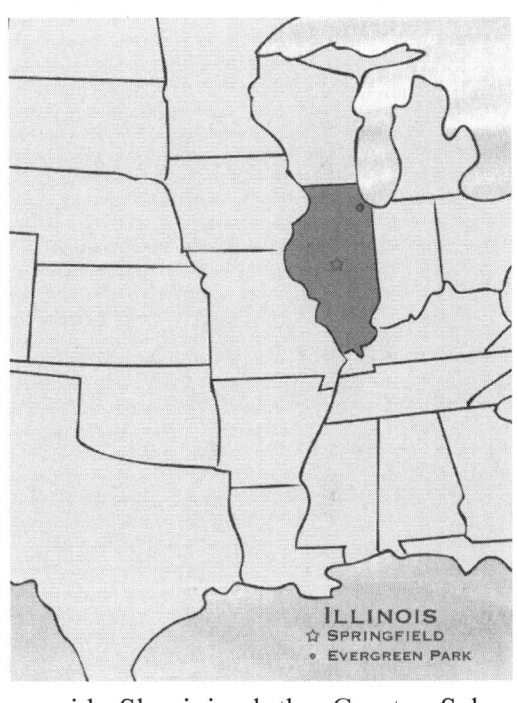

Her Aunt Duke didn't allow secular music in the house, but her cousin used to sneak records and let Mahalia listen to them. Hearing different styles of music allowed her to develop her own style, blended with the powerful sound of gospel singing.

In 1927, when Mahalia was 16 years old, she moved to Chicago and worked as a maid. She joined the Greater Salem Baptist Church choir, and her voice quickly caught the attention of others. Soon, she was working as a soloist, singing for churches across the country. Just ten years later, in 1937, she made a recording for Decca Records. Can you imagine how exciting that must have been?

Unfortunately, the record didn't sell well, and Mahalia had to get a job as a beautician. Her voice continued to gain her popularity, however, and soon she had a new contract with Apollo

Records, which lasted from 1946 to 1954. When she moved to Columbia Records, from 1954 to 1967, her career really took off.

She could be heard on the radio and television, and she performed concerts around the world! How would you like to sing to packed audiences in Europe like she did? She even got to sing for President Dwight Eisenhower and at President John F. Kennedy's inaugural ball in 1960.

Mahalia thought singing was the most fun career anybody could have, but she also wanted to use her voice for good causes. She was involved in the Civil Rights Movement with Dr. Martin Luther King Jr., singing before his famous "I Have a Dream" speech and also at his funeral five years later. She knew that singing the gospel songs that she loved would have the power to change the world in positive ways and touch people's hearts.

Anna realized that, if she wanted to get to be like Mahalia Jackson, she couldn't be afraid to sing the kind of songs she loved to sing. She couldn't limit herself to only singing the kind of songs she thought people wanted her to. She had to sing the songs that were in her heart.

"Hey, where are you going?" Miguel asked as his sister ran out of the room.

"I've got an audition to get to!" she called over her shoulder. "I'm going to sing my favorite gospel song just like Mahalia Jackson would have done!"

Bibliography:

"Mahalia Jackson." *Women in History*. October 16, 2012. <www.lkwdpl.org/wihohio/jack-mah.htm>

Speaking Up about Reaching Out

History: Sarah Grimke was born on November 26, 1792, and her sister Angelina was born February 20, 1805. They were both born in Charleston, South Carolina and grew up to become abolitionists. They are noted for being among the first women to

speak out publically for social reform and the end of slavery. Sarah died on December 23, 1873, having lived to the age of 81. Her sister Angelina Grimke died on October 26, 1879, having lived to the age of 74. Read their story to learn what we all should know about speaking out for equality.

Jake and Marissa always brought their lunch to school in a fancy lunch box. They sat with other kids who had fancy lunch boxes too. One day, a boy who had a hot lunch tray from the cafeteria wanted to sit with them.

"This table is only for kids with a lunch box!" one boy named Cody said. "Go eat your lunch over there with the other kids who get hot lunch!"

Jake looked at Cody and said, "Why did you say that? Anybody can eat at any table they want. He could have sat here with us."

"I know." Cody said, rudely. "But I don't want anybody who is different to sit by me."

Jake and Marissa thought that was horribly unfair. They decided to make buttons that said, "Everybody's a Friend." The next day at school, they wore their buttons and made an effort to sit with other kids at lunch. They sat with boys and girls from other tables. Some of them had hot lunch trays, some of them had their lunches in brown paper sacks, and some of them had lunch boxes. They were all very nice, and they all had a good time eating and then playing together at recess. Cody, however, did not look happy about it.

Marissa and Jake wanted everybody at school to treat each other fairly, with respect and kindness. They were a little like the Grimke sisters. Have you ever heard of them? Angelina and Sarah Grimke were two sisters who lived in South Carolina in the early 1800s. Their father was a judge and owned a plantation. He had many slaves and the sisters hated to watch the way they were mistreated. They spoke out against slavery every chance they could and were forced to move to the North because of their opinion.

In the North, they continued to speak against slavery, and Angelina wrote a letter that was published in a newspaper called *The Liberator* in 1836. Angelina then wrote a pamphlet called *An Appeal to the Christian Women of the South,* 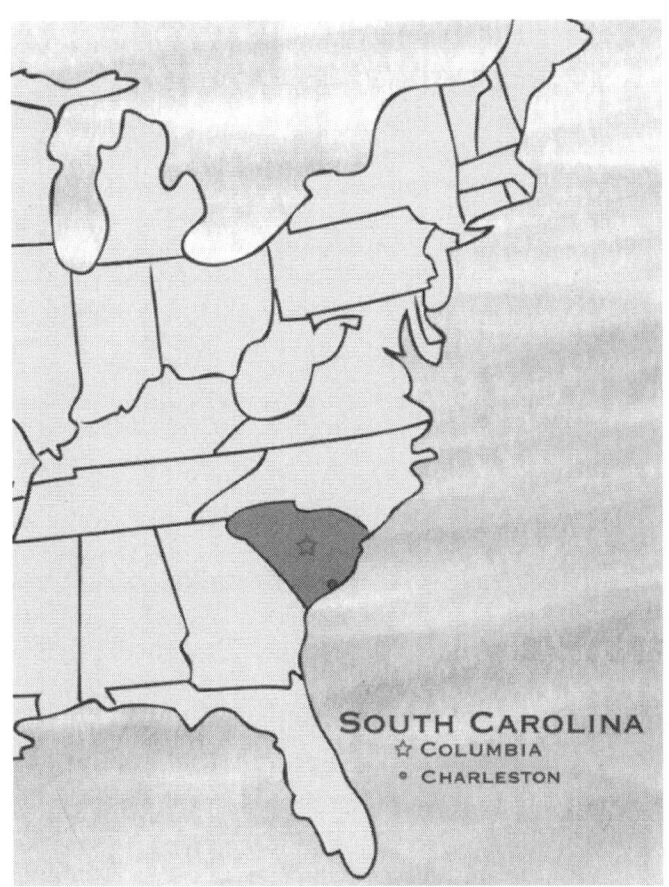 asking them to join her in ending slavery. Officials in the South became so angry over it that they burned copies of the pamphlet and warned the Grimke sisters that they would be arrested if they ever came back to the South. Can you imagine never being able to see your family or friends like that?

The sisters would not be intimidated. They knew they had to stand up for what was right and continued speaking out against slavery by giving lectures. In 1838, Angelina Grimke spoke to the

Massachusetts State Legislature, making her the first woman to address a legislative body.

Jake and Marissa knew that they had to be like the Grimke sisters and try to convince their friends to do what they knew was right and treat everyone fairly.

That night, they made enough buttons for everyone in their class and brought them to school with them the next day. Many kids were happy to take a button and made an effort to make new friends at lunch. Cody, however, still refused. He insisted that he only wanted to eat lunch with people who had a lunch box like him. What do you think you would have done?

It didn't take long before Cody was sitting all alone at lunch. Everyone had learned how fun it was to make friends with new people and treat each other kindly.

One day, Jake and Marissa came and sat down next to Cody.

"What do you want?" Cody said suspiciously.

Marissa handed him a button and said, "Everybody's a friend. That includes you, me, and everybody. Come eat with us today and play with us on the playground.

Cody joined Jake and Marissa and was pleased to discover that they were right. It didn't matter if the other kids had a lunchbox like him. It only mattered that he treated them with respect, kindness, and an open heart.

Bibliography:

"Angelina Grimke." *Peace Garden*. October 16, 2012.
<www.fresnostate.edu/peacegarden/nominees/grimke.htm>

Dyslexia Doesn't Have to Hold You Back

History: Nelson Rockefeller was born on July 8, 1908 in Bar Harbor, Maine. Although never diagnosed with it, modern experts suspect he may have had dyslexia. Despite difficulties reading, he became a very accomplished politician, serving as the forty ninth

Governor of New York from 1959 to 1973 and serving as the forty first Vice President of the U.S. from 1974 to 1977. He died on January 26, 1979 in Manhattan, New York. Hear his story and learn how having a reading disability doesn't have to hold you back from greatness.

Gabby went with her Mom and Dad to the learning center. It was the same place she had gone for all those tests last week. Her teacher had recommended they come here for an evaluation when Gabby kept struggling with her class work and getting poor grades on her assignments.

"I can't do it! I'm just stupid!" Gabby had cried.

Everyone told her that wasn't true, but she didn't believe them. She was certain that's what the education therapist, Mrs. Larson, would say at the meeting they were about to have.

"Hi Gabby, It's so good to see you again" Mrs. Larson said. She shook hands with her Mom and Dad, and they all sat down at a long table together.

Mrs. Larson looked at Gabby and said, "We analyzed the results of all your evaluations, and you have dyslexia.

Gabby felt so scared. She didn't know what that meant, but it sounded really bad!

"Dyslexia is a reading disorder that causes your brain to process symbols differently. People with dyslexia are just as intelligent as everybody else, but, because their brain is processing words differently, they often do poorly in school. We will teach you strategies to make reading easier for you and teach you how to learn in ways that work with your dyslexia."

186

Gabby breathed a sigh of relief. That didn't sound so bad. She had been afraid that she just wasn't smart, and now she knew that wasn't true. She just needed to use different strategies for reading and learning.

"You know, some very important people have had dyslexia," Mrs. Larson said.

"Really?" Gabby asked with interest.

"Yes, and one of them even went on to become the Vice President of the United States. His name was Nelson Rockefeller."

MAINE
☆ AUGUSTA
○ BAR HARBOR

"I've heard of the Rockefeller family!" Gabby said. "Didn't one of them become very wealthy as an oil tycoon?"

"Yes, Nelson's grandfather was the famous John D. Rockefeller who founded Standard Oil.

"Nelson Rockefeller was born on July 8, 1908 in Bar Harbor, Maine. He was a poor reader in school, often confusing words and numbers. Doctors didn't realize at the time that he had dyslexia. He discovered ways to improve his reading and worked hard at it. He did so well that he got accepted to Dartmouth College.

"Nelson never let his dyslexia hold him back. In 1959, he was elected as governor of New York. He was so good at his job that he got elected to four terms, serving until 1973!

"On December 19, 1974, Nelson Rockefeller became the forty first vice president of the United States, under President Gerald Ford. He decided not to run in the next election, but in 1977 he was given the Presidential Medal of Freedom award. Not too bad for someone who had started out struggling with dyslexia, is it?"

Gabby realized that, if one man could do all that, then she could do anything in life she put her mind to! She worked hard at learning the strategies they taught at the learning center. It wasn't always easy, and sometimes she felt frustrated, but soon she was seeing a real improvement in her grades. It allowed her to see that the things she was doing really were working and encouraged her to keep trying harder. When the semester came to an end, Gabby received a special award from her teacher for being the "Most Improved" student in the class. It made her feel really glad that she'd worked so hard, and she knew that having dyslexia wasn't going to hold her back from reaching all her dreams.

Bibliography:

"Nelson Rockefeller." *New World Encyclopedia.* October 19, 2012.
<http://www.newworldencyclopedia.org/entry/Nelson_Rockefeller>

Write About Your Life

History: Mary Boykin Miller was born on March 31, 1823 in Stateburg, South Carolina. Her mother was Mary Boykin, and her father was Stephen Decatur Miller, a U.S. Representative and later Governor of South Carolina. When she was 17, she married James

Chestnut Jr. on April 23, 1840. Her book Mary Chesnut's Civil War *(1981) won the Pulitzer Prize in 1982 and has been lauded as the most important work by a Confederate author. She died on November 22, 1886. Her story is an inspiration for anyone who has ever kept a diary and even for those who haven't yet, but will.*

"Okay class, I want all of you to begin keeping a journal every day," Mrs. Nelson said to her students. "You can write about things that you've done, feelings you have, your hopes and dreams, or anything you want. Just make sure you write at least one page a day."

Sarah and Elizabeth were twin sisters who both had Mrs. Nelson for their teacher. Sarah grabbed her new empty journal and hugged it to her chest. "I love journaling! This assignment is going to be so fun and easy! I'm going to start writing right now!"

Elizabeth rolled her eyes at her sister. She couldn't have felt more differently if she tried. She hated journaling. She didn't understand why anyone should have to write down the things they had done that day or how they felt about it. Who could possibly care?

Luckily, a woman named Mary Boykin Miller Chestnut hadn't felt like Elizabeth. Mary Miller had been born in the South on March 31, 1923 on her grandparents' plantation near Stateburg, South Carolina. Her father was a state senator and became Governor of South Carolina when Mary was just five years old.

When she was seventeen, she married James Chestnut Jr. He later became a U.S. Senator for the state of South Carolina. When the Civil War broke out, he became an aide to President Jefferson Davis and fought for the Confederate Army as a Brigadier General.

Mary Chestnut began writing in a diary on February 18, 1861. She gave her impressions of events of the Civil War as they were happening. She wasn't afraid to write about things that many people didn't want to talk about, like when men had children with their women slaves and how much she hated slavery. She wanted people to know what life was really like in the South and not just make everything sound nice. She was willing to write about the way things were, as she saw them.

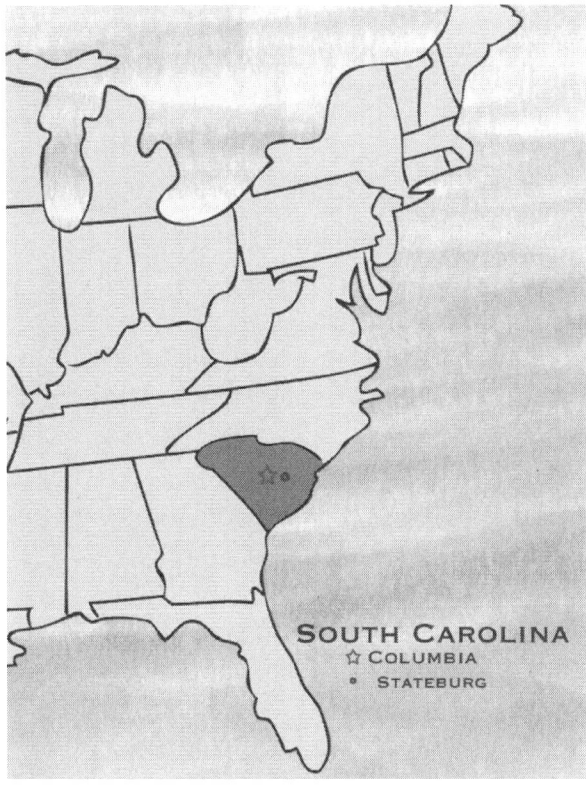

SOUTH CAROLINA
☆ COLUMBIA
● STATEBURG

She ended her diary on June 26, 1865 and realized it was something she wanted others to read. She spent a lot of time editing it and making it as accurate and detailed as possible.

Many years later, in 1981, her diary was published under the title *Mary Chestnuts' Civil War*. It was a powerful account of American history, and she won the Pulitzer Prize for it in 1982.

Sarah wanted to write about her life, just like Mary Chestnut had. Every evening before she went to bed, she pulled out her journal and wrote all the events of the day, her impressions, and how she felt about it.

Her sister Elizabeth wasn't wild about the assignment from their teacher and dreaded doing it. It felt silly to write about the boring things she did each day. She started writing silly jokes and stories in her journal to make it more interesting.

One day, something really funny happened at lunch, and Elizabeth thought, "I'll have to write about this in my journal!" Soon, she started finding more things that happened during her day that she wanted to write about.

Mrs. Nelson wrote comments in her journal when she read her stories. One time she wrote "So funny! You have a great sense of humor!"

Sarah continued to write in her journal with a serious attitude. She liked to detail important events and how she felt about them. Elizabeth found she enjoyed writing in her journal with a light heart, full of humor and funny stories.

Maybe one day, they'll look back on their journals and enjoy reading all the things they had written. Who knows – maybe one day they'll grow up to find they recorded something important that they'll want others to read. Do you keep a journal or diary? If you don't, maybe you should try. If you already do, keep on writing. You never know what you may see.

Bibliography:

"Mary Boykin Chestnut." *New World Encyclopedia*. October 19, 2012. <http://www.newworldencyclopedia.org/entry/Mary_Boykin_Chesnut>

Through the Clouds

History: Amelia Earhart was born on July 24, 1897 in Atchison, Kansas. She was the first woman to fly solo across the Atlantic Ocean and set many aviation records. She disappeared on July 2, 1937 at the age of 39, when attempting to fly around the

world. Her love of flying is contagious, even today. See how her story helps a young boy learn to conquer his fears and develop a love for traveling.

Emma and her younger brother, Dylan, were going on a trip to visit their grandparents who lived in another state far away. Where do your grandparents live?

It was a very long drive to get there, so Emma and Dylan were going to get to ride on an airplane. Emma had been on an airplane before, and she was very happy and excited, but this would be Dylan's first time, and he was very scared. He didn't want to go. Have you ever felt that way?

They checked their suitcases in at the front counter and got their tickets. Then they had to stand in line to go through the metal detector. They each had a backpack full of toys to take on the plane, and they had to put them through an x-ray machine.

Mom and Dad were able to go with them to the airplane gate, but they weren't going with them on the plane. Emma and Dylan would be flying by themselves. The more Dylan thought about it, the more scared he felt. Emma, however, wasn't afraid at all. She was happy and looking forward to the trip. Dylan tried to be brave just like her.

The flight attendant was a very nice woman named Sharon. They got to be the first people to board the plane. Sharon guided them to their seats and helped them put their backpacks in a safe place. She showed them how to work their seatbelts and tray tables and how to push the button to call for help.

"Don't worry. You're going to have a great flight, and I'll be coming check on you once we get up in the air." Sharon said. She could see that Dylan was feeling nervous.

Emma could see it too and wanted to help her little brother know that everything was going to be all right.

"Flying is really fun." Emma comforted him. "Let's pretend like we're famous aviators! I'll be Amelia Earhart, and you can be Fred Noonan!"

"Who are they?" asked Dylan.

Emma answered saying, "Amelia Earhart was a famous pilot who broke lots of records in the skies.

"She was born in Atchison, Kansas on July 24, 1897. When she wasn't working at her job as a nurse, she loved to watch airplane stunt shows. One day, she took a ten minute ride in a plane and decided then and there that she would learn how to fly.

"She worked hard to save up the $1000 she needed for flying lessons, and she soon became a pilot. After that, she continued to save money until she was able to buy her own plane!

"Amelia had a great time flying, and in 1928 she got a terrific opportunity. Captain Hilton H. Railey asked her to join pilots Wilmer Stultz and Louis Gordon on a flight they were taking across the Atlantic Ocean, from the U.S. to England. Their plane was called the *Friendship*. What would you name your airplane if you had one?

"Amelia agreed to go, and, on June 17 and 18, 1928, she became the first woman to cross the Atlantic. Even though she was just a passenger on the flight, the event made her famous.

"She became even more famous in May 1932 when she crossed the Atlantic completely by herself. She even set a new record with the flight by completing the journey in just 13 hours and 30 minutes. President Herbert Hoover gave her a special medal for it.

"A few years later, she became the first woman to fly the difficult route from California to Hawaii."

"That's all really cool!" Dylan said. "You can pretend to be Amelia Earhart, but what about me? Who can I pretend to be?"

"You can pretend to be Fred Noonan. He was an expert navigator who had a distinguished career chartering flights across the Pacific Ocean. Having a good navigator is very important to a pilot.

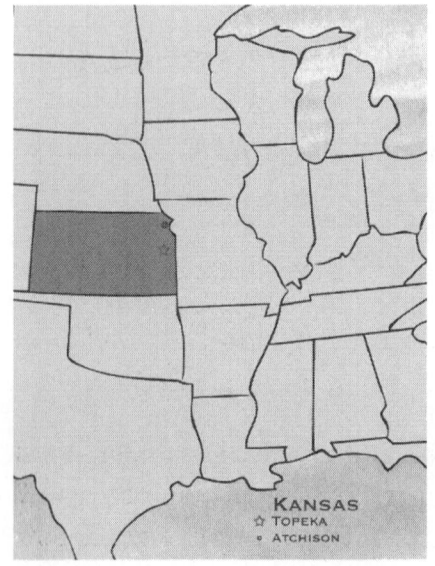

"In June 1937, Fred Noonan and Amelia Earhart set out to make a historic flight around the world. Their plane became lost after they left New Guinea, and no one has ever found what happened to them."

"You mean they disappeared forever?" Dylan was entranced.

"They were declared dead, but no one will ever know what really happened."

"That's so cool!" Dylan said feeling excited. Then he became worried. "Do you think that will happen to us on this plane?"

"Definitely not!" Emma exclaimed with confidence. "There have been a lot of advances in airplanes since the 1930s. Planes today are very safe and equipped with lots of tracking equipment. When you fly on a plane today, you know you are in good hands."

The pilot announced that it was time for takeoff. Dylan leaned back in his seat and looked out the window. He could see the scenery outside moving faster and faster as the plane rolled down the runway.

Suddenly, the plane lifted off the ground, and Dylan could feel that they flying! He understood why Amelia Earhart loved it so much. After a while, the flight attendant came and offered him some juice and a snack. He played games with Emma, and, before he knew it, the flight was over and it was time to land.

Dylan and Emma had to wait for all the other passengers to get off the plane first, so the flight attendant could help them off the plane. Grandma and Grandpa were waiting for them and greeted them both with a big hug.

"So what did you think of your first plane ride?" Grandma asked Dylan.

"I loved it! I think I'm going to be a world traveler when I grow up, just like Amelia Earhart!"

"I thought you were afraid to travel." Emma teased.

"Not anymore." Dylan said proudly. "I see now that traveling to new places is a lot of fun and nothing to be afraid of at all!"

Have you ever traveled some place far away like Dylan and Emma? Have you ever traveled on a bus, train, boat, or plane? Which one do you think would be the most fun? No matter how you get there, traveling to faraway places can be a wonderful adventure.

Bibliography:

"Amelia Earhart." *Pitara Kids Network*. October 12, 2012.
<www.pitara.com/magazine/people/online.asp?story=47>

Eisenhower and the Interstate Highway System

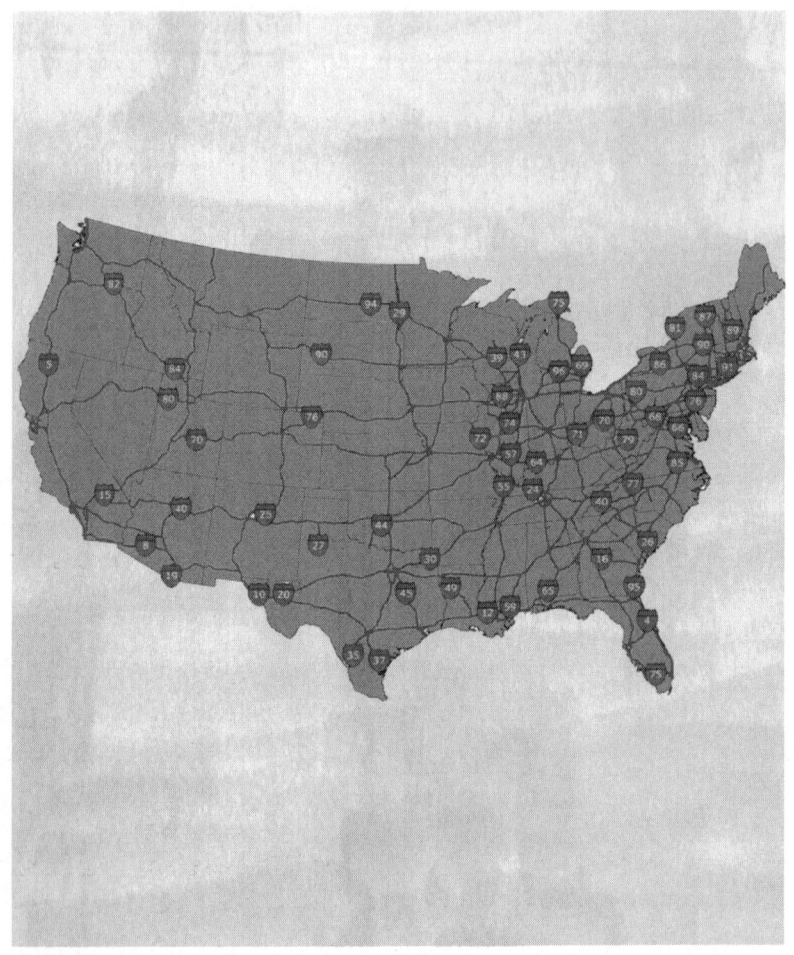

History: The National Interstate Highway System of the United States is a network of freeways, highways and beltways that span the entire country. It was instituted by President Dwight D. Eisenhower with the Federal Aid Highway Act of 1956. Today it is over 47,000 miles long and has been hailed as the largest public works program in our nation's history.

Jake and Jenny had just finished packing their suitcases for their big family vacation. Mom said "Did you remember to pack everything you need?"

Jake knew that he had packed his most comfortable clothes and some of his favorite toys. Jenny knew she had backed her special stuffed teddy bear and her fluffy slipper.

"Yes Mom" they both said together.

Mom said, "Did you remember to pack socks and a warm sweater?"

Both Jenny and Jake realized they had not, and shook their heads.

Mom said, "You need to make a list of all the things you need on your vacation. If the list is too big and everything won't fit, you need to prioritize the list and make sure to pack the most important things first." What would you prioritize on a big trip?

Jake and Jenny repacked their suitcases, making sure to pack socks and a warm sweater as their first priority, and saving fun things like toys and fluffy slippers as a low priority and packing them last.

After Mom checked their suitcases, Dad loaded them into the trunk of the car and they all took their seats. As Dad drove the car up the onramp onto the interstate highway, the whole family felt like their journey had officially begun. Have you ever taken a long car trip with your family?

Jenny and Jake looked out their windows. There were lots of cars all traveling at fast speeds down the smooth concrete highway. Out the windows they could see buildings and trees whizzing by. As they left the city, they saw great fields of farmland and occasional barns dotting the countryside. When they grew bored, they began to play games looking for letters of the alphabet on signs. Next, they started looking for numbers.

It didn't take long for Jake to notice certain pattern in the numbers on the interstate signs. He called up to the front seat of the car "Hey Dad, why do all the highways that go from East to West have numbers that are even and all the ones that go from North to South have numbers that are odd?"

"That's a great question" Dad said, "You should ask Eisenhower, it was his idea to make them that way."

"Who's that?" Jake asked.

"Eisenhower was a five-star general who became the 34th president of the United States. He was one of our greatest leaders and is credited with instituting our country's Interstate Highway System."

Jenny rolled her eyes and said, "You make it sound like building a highway was as important as being a general or being the president. Why would anyone care if he built a highway when he had done so many other great things?"

This time Mom answered by saying "Building an international highway system was pretty great. In fact, many have viewed it as this country's greatest public works project ever made."

"Why?" Jake and Jenny both asked together.

Mom handed them a map she'd been holding. She said "Just look at this map. See what a huge distance it is from one part of the United States to another? Imagine having to travel across this country with no highway system. Imagine if there were only dirt roads and wooden bridges?"

Jake and Jenny both tried to imagine what that would be like. It would be bumpy with some places having mud you would sink in

200

or rocks you couldn't travel over. Can you imagine how difficult that would be?

Dad said "Just after WWI, the Secretary of War, Newton D. Baker, ordered a committee investigation, to see if our military forces would be able to travel across the United States with heavy trucks full of soldiers and supplies. Eisenhower was part of part of this committee. Baker wanted to know if our country would be able to defend itself if there was ever a war on American soil. The reports came back that most of our roads could not handle heavy trucks and that they would not be able to travel fast enough or far enough to do any good.

Not long afterwards, our country got involved in WWII. Eisenhower was chosen by President Roosevelt as Supervisor, leading troops through Africa and across Europe. Our soldiers had to struggle with getting tanks and trucks full of supplies across difficult areas where the roads were useless. Then, they had the pleasure of passing effortlessly along the smooth roadways of the Audubon in Germany, which is like a highway. It made it clear to the President that having a highway system across the United States was very important for our country's defense.

When Eisenhower was elected our nation's 34th president in 1953, he made building a National Highway Defense System (NHDS) one of his priorities. That means it was really important to him and he wanted to do it as soon as possible. What is something that is a priority for you? Doing your homework before you play? Eating your vegetables so you can have desert? Setting priorities is a good way to make sure important things get done first.

On June 29, Eisenhower signed the Federal-Aid Highway Act of 1956, which guaranteed funding for the NHDS. It was a truly wondrous project for its time, and still is today because of the massive size of it.

Starting in Florida with I-4 and I-10, and ending with the longest part of the NHDS is the I-90, which stretches more than 3,000 miles from Boston to Seattle the even numbered highways travels from East to West. In contrast, it is the uneven numbered highways that travels from North to South, starting with I-5 in California and ending with I-95 which travels down the East coast, passing through fifteen states and the District of Columbia. When you see any three digit number like I-295 which is in Jacksonville, Florida, you can know that these are beltways. A beltways is an interstate which travels around a major cities and interconnects with the rest of the Interstate system.

In some places the NHDS travels along the coastline, offering beautiful scenery. In other places, it crosses over huge bodies of water or is suspended in the air by cables and in some instances even go underwater. It is indeed a wonder of engineering.

The NHDS is constantly growing and being improved, with many communities looking for ways to make their highways 'green' or friendly to the environment." Dad said.

Jake said "Is that why they planted all those trees along the highway at our house?"

"Yes." Mom said "It's also why they built that bridge over the river where the wild deer like to drink, instead of having the new onramp just cut right through the wildlife land."

Jenny said, "We learned in school that some communities make landmarks and monuments near highways so that more people can enjoy them. We saw pictures of the Great Platte River Road Archway Monument in Kearney, Nebraska. It straddles the highway, resembling a giant covered bridge, to honor the pioneers. It was amazing!"

Dad said "The NHDS had a lot of amazing and positive effects for Americans beyond Eisenhower's purpose of defense. Can you name some of the ways it has improved America?"

Jenny cried out "People can use it to travel easily for their daily lives, like going to work or visiting grandma's!"

Jake said "It also helps commerce, by allowing businesses to ship goods all across the country with ease!"

People can visit their families more, rather than travel on planes. Can you think of other ways that our highway system helps Americans?

Jake and Jenny spent the rest of the car ride thinking of all the great things that our Highway System helps make life better for Americans everywhere. They were glad that building it had been a priority for President Eisenhower.

Bibliography:

U.S. History, America's Interstate Highway System viewed November 26, 212 at http://www.historynet.com/president-dwight-eisenhower-and-americas-interstate-highway-system.htm

The End

ArisePublishing.com

About the Authors:

Mickey and Cavélle Roman, having their own business and also being missionaries, have a passion to see the moral value of today's culture upheld and in an effort to make their contribution they have released this book.

Visit *arisepublishing.com* to see companion books and more book titles.

Printed in Great Britain
by Amazon.co.uk, Ltd.,
Marston Gate.